OLLI@UGA
Memoir-Writing Group

2020

Stories are copyright © 2020 OLLI Memoir Writers. All rights reserved.

No part of this book, either text or image, may be reproduced or used in any manner whatsoever without the express written permission of the author(s).

Printed and bound in the United States of America

Cover illustration by Linda Koehler
Design and edits by Elizabeth Carleton
Stories, photographs, and illustrations contributed by members of the *Writing Memoir* Special Interest Group, Osher Lifelong Learning Institute, University of Georgia.

Trade paperback edition:
ISBN-13: 978-0-578-70903-1

CONTRIBUTORS

Glenn Ames
Roger Bailey
Robert Alan Black
Susan Brassard
Connie Crawley
Peggy Harrington
Richard Horner
Sharon Hughes
Linda Jones Jenkins
Terry Kaley
Tom Kenyon
Nancy MacNair
Jim Marshall
Janet Martin
JES Mason
Alice Mohor
AC "Charles" Wilmoth
DeAnne Wilmoth

Foreword
Writing Memoir

I'm amazed at how much I learn from myself. Or at least, momentarily, think I learn. My youth saw me as the cosmic center of everything. Every once in a while, this twenty-two-year-old narcissism flashes as a presence in my seventy-six-year-old body and mind. I can go out in an afternoon to feel

>Cosmically important—
>>find a parking spot
>>before the door
>>go in to eat
>>please someone
>>leave with a smile
>>a third latte
>>and a scone–
>>*on the house–*
>
>Gently cool
>>the day can wrap me
>>in a breezy sunshine
>>as I drive off
>>in my corolla
>>feeling the light
>>glowing within–
>
>Cosmically important

Of course, this ingenuous perspective as the cosmic center of it all is common to human beings. As youngsters, we'd accomplish little if we felt ourselves to be inconsequential, if we let our miniscule presence on this Earth overwhelm our sense of wonder and limit our personal promise. As I age, I learn, I discover and I find a wisdom that connects me to an increasingly awe-inspiring world, to those I like and love, and to myself, as one still growing to discover himself. The American poet Robert Frost penned that often "the afternoon knows what the morning never suspected." A while back, I wanted to change a point of view I expressed in a poem written when I was sixty-two. But…that was me then. I knew to leave it alone.

I am a pre-millennial library. My inner technology, however, is challenged by a neurological and a physical obsolescence increasingly beyond my control no matter the tai chi, the meditation, the YMCA exercise room. These certainly help maintain my physical and mental acuity, but ultimately aging's relentless emergence will make me fold my tent and steal away, but not before I revisit photographs, rub my fingers over valued objects, plumb still-existing social issues, eat Mother's plum pie and look closely at important life events through the years that have brought me some wisdom. A variety of expected and unexpected challenges have taught me that frequently to live is to suffer; to survive is to find some meaning in the suffering. To find some meaning involves encountering pain alien to experience. That is life.

It is healthy to read letters from years past; to watch movies with Charles Chaplin and Bette Davis; to reflect on who I was in 1968 when I found *2001: A Space Odyssey* so mindblowing; to revisit Neal Armstrong's monumental steps on the moon in 1969; to reflect on the presence of racism, sexism and homophobia in my own identity; to retrieve scents and tastes that return me to an apple tree on Division Street where my friend John Britton lived; and slowly to uncover a menu of moments that I want to explore – and then to share – with those I love…

Roger D. Bailey,
OLLI@UGA Facilitator
February 18, 2020

In my forties, as my friend Franklin photographed me on our wondrous trip to Monticello.

Welcome to the world of memoir.

Portrait of Roger Bailey by Katherine Pflegar
In the fashion of Chuck Close
2004

Contents

Glenn Ames …   Building Latrines in Santa Elena:
Tales of a Peace Corps Volunteer in Venezuela
… 1

Travels in Ukraine and the Workers' Paradise Hotel
… 7

Roger Bailey …   Nature's Flit
… 15

Music and the Early Days…
… 17

Robert Alan Black …   4 Prisons in 5+ Years:
Surviving to Move On to a Life of Value Once Again
… 21

Susan Brassard …   Cars
… 27

Connie Crawley …   I Married a Model
… 33

The Beak Girl
… 37

Peggy Harrington …   Milo
… 41

Richard Horner ... Untitled
... 45

Sharon Hughes ... Holes in the Yard
... 47
The Dirt Tracks of New York State
... 49

Linda Jones Jenkins ... I Finally Got My Nickel
... 55

Terry Kaley ... Sinking Holiday Spirits
... 61

Tom Kenyon ... Mother Buys a House
... 65

Nancy MacNair ... Adopting Kathleen
... 71

Jim Marshall ... Destination Vacation
... 79

Janet Martin ... On Her Own
... 83

JES Mason ... Ours Is a Literate Family
... 87
Comfort in the Time of the Pandemic
... 93

Alice Mohor … s.s. devonshire 1851
… 95
christmas stollen
… 97
sunday dinner
… 99
electric lawn mower
… 101
35 mm slides
… 103
old barney
… 105

AC "Charles" Wilmoth … Uncle Arthur Comes to Visit
… 107

DeAnne Wilmoth … Under Thy Sheltering Arms
… 113

Building Latrines in Santa Elena: Tales of a Peace Corps Volunteer in Venezuela

by Glenn Ames

"Where is the owner of this house?" yelled the Inspector of Latrines as we finalized the inspection of the newly constructed latrine. He had discovered that the owner had put a lock on the latrine door and no one could use it. "Who has the key?" demanded the inspector. "He has it," responded the housewife. "Where is he?" demanded the inspector. "He is in the mountains picking coffee," responded the woman, whereupon the inspector seized a hammer and proceeded to smash the lock off the door. To his astonishment, the farmer had stored his most prized possessions, his saddle, mule harness, and tools, in the latrine and locked the door to protect them from thieves and the weather. We discovered that culture and perceptions had a lot more to do with the success of public health campaigns to fight hookworm and other diseases in this poor, rural farming community in Venezuela than just the construction of concrete outhouses.

The story of our public health campaign began with Nia, my Peace Corps colleague, and me meeting the local home economist, Maria. She was charged with organizing 5-V Clubs for rural schools in our area and she invited us to help her organize 4-H type clubs in these rural schools. Since she did not have a car, nor could she drive, I was invited to chauffeur Maria and Nia in the Ministry of Agriculture's jeep up rocky, winding, one-lane roads to Santa Elena.

In the program, Nia taught the girls how to knit sweaters while I worked with the boys to build coffee nurseries, beehives, and other simple projects. At the end of the afternoon session, we played volleyball with the kids. But we soon discovered that there were no latrines in Santa Elena or in other rural schools where we worked. We had to "hold it," as we drove down the bumpy road to town. More than once Nia yelled at me from the back of the jeep, "Can't you go any faster? I can't hold it much longer."

Further evidence of the need for better sanitation came from the mounds of old lab reports I found in the back of the abandoned hospital where I lived in town. Thirty percent of the lab reports showed patients with hookworm and other intestinal diseases. Furthermore, the periodic attacks of Montezuma's revenge we all experienced underscored the need for better sanitation.

Eventually, we discovered that there was a division of the Ministry of Public Health that built latrines, but it was located over the mountains in the city of El Vigía, the Dodge City at the southern end of Lake Maracaibo. The challenge was how to entice the public health officials to come to Santa Elena, which was well out of their zone of operations. A Peace Corps couple had tried to work with them, but the project failed; they gave up and returned to the U.S. Our Peace Corps rep also told me that this agency was difficult to work with and that we should not try it. However, we had to find some solution to the lack of sanitation in the village or we could not work there.

During our Peace Corps training at the University of Denver, our community development instructor taught us that we should organize the community, take a delegation of our respective clients – in this case *campesinos* – to the ministry, and demand action on our needs. Thus, we organized a group of *campesinos* to go with me to the ministry and request that a latrine-building project be started in our community.

Clearly, the "*jefe*" of the sanitation department did not want a delegation of peasant farmers in his office, where the air conditioner had been turned down to just above freezing, a common occurrence in very important bureaucratic offices. Moreover, he had had a terrible experience with other volunteers who tried to work with his department. He unceremoniously threw us out of his office. Dejected, we climbed into the jeep and started the long trip back to Santa Elena. But we could not give up.

Clearly a delegation of peasants was not going to work. I decided to try a different tactic. I recalled that the first time I met the *jefe*, I had taken along a female volunteer, stationed in El Vigía, with me to help translate. The *jefe* had taken a special interest in her and the meeting had gone well, although no promises of support were made. The next time I went I invited Marjorie, a volunteer stationed with us in Tovar, to go along with me to see the *jefe*. She impressed the *jefe* with her attractiveness, poise and stature, but still no commitment. On subsequent trips to see the *jefe*, I took different female Peace Corps volunteers with me; a total of five in all. Apparently the *jefe* was impressed with my *machismo* and the persistence paid off. The *jefe* agreed to send his inspector to survey Santa Elena, mark the houses, and help us organize the latrine-building project.

Nia and I decided to move to Santa Elena temporarily to oversee the project. We moved in with Don Pablo, who, we later discovered, was the home economist's father and the local moneylender. Don Pablo's house was tumbling down over his head. The first two rooms had leaky roofs. Nevertheless, we used them to store the concrete latrine floors and roofs, cinder blocks for the walls, and sheet metal doors. Don Pablo lived alone but two orphan boys, Geronimo and Miguel, stayed with him to chop wood, cook, and milk the cows. A partially domesticated wild pig roamed through the open patio. The kitchen was a mess; there were no windows, only two open doors. The walls were covered with black soot due to decades of cooking over an open wood fire. Smoke filtered out through holes in the rafters but when the wind blew hard, everyone made a hasty retreat from the smoke-filled room until it cleared out.

Don Pablo also cured his "*queso criollo*" or local cheese on two planks hanging from the rafters over the wood fire. It was the most unsanitary situation for dairy products I ever saw. There were insects everywhere in the rafters in addition to a constant shower of dirt falling from the adobe material that held the roof tiles in place. I got sick every time a *campesino* family offered me a slice of this local delicacy; it was a petri dish full of bacteria that would tear the insides out of the toughest, unsuspecting Yankee who ate it.

Building our latrine took on a heightened sense of urgency under these circumstances. The orphan boys and I started digging the pit for the latrine in the middle of a banana grove not far from Don Pablo's house. The inspector insisted on a two-meter-deep pit but we gave up after a meter and a half; the rocks were too solid and we could not go any deeper. That night, John, another volunteer, helped me pour the concrete base by the light of a gas lantern. No one in the village had ever seen men work at night because there wasn't any electricity in the village; our work became a big source of gossip in the community. After the cement hardened, I laid the concrete block walls. Unfortunately, I did not allow for a roof overhang. However, the concrete slab stayed in place anyway. I attached the sheet metal door and we were in business.

Building the latrines was not the end of the project. The ministry's inspector insisted that everyone give a stool sample, which I would take to the local hospital lab for analysis. My Spanish had improved but I was challenged when I had to explain to illiterate peasant families what the plastic containers were for and that I would be back in the morning to collect them for the lab. Even more surprising was the shock on the lab technician's face when I brought him a bag of 50 stool samples and the promise that I would be back next week and the week after that with another batch.

In the end, the villagers never received the medicine they needed for intestinal parasites. The inspector had no power over the local hospital, so that part of the project didn't get done. We completed 125 latrines and there was need for many more because families who lived farther up the hillside were not included in our project's survey. The sanitation department's *jefe* was very pleased that we completed so many latrines for his reports; I became a good friend, or *compadre*, of the inspector as he made his final inspections. Besides the locked doors and concrete slabs being used as wash boards, we found other examples of people using the latrines to store their belongings and continue their previous unsanitary practices of going behind the rock walls at night. The saga of our latrine project involved a mixture of politics, public health campaigns, misguided enthusiasm, and cultural misunderstanding in rural Venezuela. In the end, I learned how critically important understanding another culture is when creating and implementing any project that is intended to change people's behavior.

Glenn C.W. Ames
Professor Emeritus
University of Georgia

Digging through rock to form the latrine pit.

Laying cinder block walls with one of the orphan boys.

Travels in Ukraine and the Workers' Paradise Hotel
by Glenn Ames

If you want to stay out of trouble in the post-Soviet world, the first valuable Russian word to learn is "*Nyet,*" as my wife and I discovered when we were attending a conference on land ownership in Kiev, Ukraine, in the early 1990s. After a long flight from the U.S., we arrived in Kiev and passed through customs, met our hosts, and boarded our bus to the dachas where former communist party bosses stayed during important committee meetings in Soviet times. No hotels were open or functioning at this time. We had selected the dachas for our accommodations during the conference because the other housing options were not very appealing; they were old college dormitories on campus or small residences. Maybe we had selected more than we bargained for!

At the guardhouse entrance to the "dachas in the woods," there were no smiling, bilingual receptionists to take our documents and issue us our room keys. Instead armed guards reviewed our names on the list of conference attendees, stamped some papers, and instructed the bus driver to proceed into the woods where our accommodations were located. At the bus turnaround, our host and translator issued us keys, showed us the path through the woods where we could find our dacha, told us when the bus would return, and bid us good evening. Kathie and I hauled our luggage up the path to our side of the duplex and went inside.

The décor was early 1900s Czarist or Bolshevik chic. We had a bedroom, bathroom and kitchen. The walls were two feet thick with double or triple windows that had long been painted shut. After we unloaded our suitcases, I decided to go outside and look around before the sun went down. What a mistake! The instant I opened the door a loud alarm bell sounded and a flashing red light came on. Then an armed guard came running, shouting, "*Nyet! Nyet!*" and gesturing that I should go back inside. Apparently, once inside, you were forbidden to leave until the next morning. The rules were strictly enforced. This was not the last time I would run afoul of the rules and regulations that had not changed in post-Soviet Ukraine.

Taking a shower or bath was also a new experience. I had to ignite a gas burner on the wall to warm up the frigid water that came out of the pipes. After several tries with old matches I found in the kitchen, I lit the pilot light and turned on the gas valve under the burner, which ignited with the force of a blast furnace. We were afraid of the contraption and settled for a sponge bath with water heated over the kitchen stove.

The next morning, breakfast was a new experience. Our hosts met us at the turnaround and we boarded the bus to a restaurant that had been reopened to feed the conference attendees. In lieu of coffee, we were offered shot glasses of vodka (unlimited). Tea, sugar and bread were available. Then we were served a traditional Ukrainian dish of slices of liver or kidney swimming in a gelatinous bowl of cold pork fat. No one ate it. The rest of our daily meals were taken at the conference center. After a few days, some

Italian conference attendees gave up and returned home because they could not adjust to the food and Spartan lodging accommodations.

Once the conference started, we settled into a routine of speeches and presentations. In Ukraine, a vast agricultural country the size of France, land use policy was critical to the political and economic revival of the country. Under Communist Central Planning, especially during Stalin's reign, the Communists confiscated and collectivized the land during the 1920s and '30s. Villages were consolidated into vast agricultural enterprises and all traces of private property were obliterated, creating huge fields to be farmed with heavy machinery. The collective farm became the source of employment, housing, education, healthcare, recreation, retirement benefits, and political organization, all under the tutelage of the collective farm manager. After the implosion of the Former Soviet Union (FSU) in the early 1990s, the critical question became, "Who owns the land and who has the right to use it?" We were about to find out; what an adventure this was going to be.

One of the featured speakers at the conference was a young man who had taken advantage of the new land use policy that allowed people to claim 30 hectares of land and machinery from the collective farm to start their private farms. The farmer, his father and brother each claimed 30 hectares of land and set up their farm. During the intersession of the conference, a group of us went in search of this new private farmer to see how he was doing. This was an adventure we would never forget because we came face to face with the strict enforcement of old rules and new regulations that we did not know about.

Soon it became apparent that unrestricted travel was still not possible in western Ukraine, which borders central

Europe and the gateway to the West. As we traveled down the highway, our host and travel guide, Sergei, had to stop and pay his respects to the authorities every time we crossed over into a different district. Sometimes the stops were relatively short while other times the authorities hosted us for lunch and a round of toasts to U.S.–Ukrainian friendship and cooperation.

Finally we arrived at our destination, the private farm and its owners. They were out harvesting sugar beets with their tractors and beet harvesters. We interviewed them, wanting to know how they claimed their land and machinery from the collective farm where they worked previously. Eventually it became too dark and cold to hold pen and paper; then the farmer invited us to have dinner at his father's house in the nearby village.

We were treated to a delicious dinner of pickled cabbages, boiled potatoes, beets, cucumbers, bread, and vodka. After several rounds of toasts to friendship and cooperation, we bid our hosts good evening and drove to the workers' Paradise Hotel.

The hotel was a four-story rectangular block building that had been a dormitory for workers who helped rebuild the town after WWII. Little had changed since the workers left in the late 1950s. An elderly babushka and her daughter were watching an old grainy television and barely acknowledged our presence as we lugged our luggage up the steps to the reception area. "Yes, your rooms are ready," said the proprietress. "They are freshly painted." When we climbed to the fourth floor, we discovered a bucket with a wet paint brush beside the door to our room. Apparently, they decided to paint our rooms on the day we arrived in case we canceled. Sergei asked us if we needed anything else and bid us good evening. Once my wife and I were inside our dorm room, we discovered that the beds were very narrow cots with straw for mattresses. Fresh straw at that! Men's restrooms were on the 2nd, 3rd and 4th floors; ladies' on the 1st only. Eventually we fell asleep only to be rudely awakened by the pulsating beat of a disco club only a few buildings away. The music, singing and patriotic songs went on all night. We could not close the window because the paint fumes were overwhelming.

The next morning our adventure began anew. We checked out of the hotel. Sergei told us to wait by our car and Peugeot van while he went to see the authorities and inform them that we were returning to Kiev that day but stopping at a cannery and other points of interest along the way. While everyone waited for him to return, Kathie and I wandered around the area and found a state-run grocery store and went inside. There was nothing for sale except a half-kilo of butter, a piece of cheese and hundreds of glass jars filled with gigantic cucumbers that no one wanted. I took a picture of the jars of cucumbers, and then "all Hell broke loose."

A policeman immediately appeared and demanded our documents. We only had our conference badges with us, and they were written in English. "*Nyet*," said the policemen as he became more agitated and demanded our papers, also written in English. Of course, we didn't know any Russian; however, *nyet* was clearly understood. As the situation became more heated, we eased our way to the door and started walking toward our van. The policeman followed us all the way to the car, becoming even more agitated with every step. Once we arrived at our van and car, the young drivers explained to the policeman that we were indeed conference attendees and innocent of any crimes, my photo of the giant cucumbers notwithstanding. He was still angry and told our drivers that he was going to talk to his boss about our breaking the rules of no photos of giant cucumbers or anything else.

Soon the policeman returned with his boss and again the drivers explained that we were conference attendees and meant no disrespect. He was not satisfied and more heated discussions ensued. We were getting worried that we might be arrested. Finally, Sergei returned with our travel documents, all duly stamped and signed. The policemen were satisfied and let us go on with our journey, but this was not the last time we would encounter the police that day.

About midnight our two-vehicle caravan reached the outskirts of Kiev. The highways were deserted when all of a sudden a policeman appeared at the side of the road and waved for us to stop. He demanded the driver's papers and began to check them. "*Nyet*," he exclaimed, "your documents are not in order." At this point, Sergei exited our van and tried to explain that we were conference attendees returning from a trip to the Cherkasy region of Ukraine. He was still not satisfied. Sergei asked him what could resolve the situation. The policeman explained that he had run out of gas and could not get home. If we would give him some gas, he would let us go. However, the Peugeot van ran on diesel, not gasoline. What a predicament! Since the other part of our group was in a car ahead of us, they returned to find out what our problem was.

Sergei explained that the policeman needed gas to get home. The driver said he had enough to give him and still get to our dachas. The driver drove around some bushes out of the sight of the foreigners. The policemen brought out a hose and gas can and siphoned out enough gas to get his car started. Everyone seemed happy and he allowed us to proceed on our way to our dachas. It was well after midnight when we got to our dacha. We went inside and did not open the door until the next morning, thankful that we had survived two encounters with the police in one very memorable day.

Our trip to Ukraine opened our eyes to the extremely difficult situation the Ukrainian people faced as they transitioned to a new political and economic environment. Obsolete agribusinesses and factories closed; unemployment and inflation skyrocketed; but probably the hardest adjustment was the fear and uncertainty surrounding the collapse of central planning and all that it entailed; who was in charge and who had the right to use the country's resources. The conference in Kiev was only a very tiny step in answering these momentous questions.

Glenn C.W. Ames
Professor Emeritus
University of Georgia

OLLI@UGA

Nature's Flit

Roger D. Bailey

I love my mailbox. I love the birds in Forest Heights. Through the years, I have loved their visits as they bring me to my still space.

Nature's Flit

in the sun
up and down
the little bird
on the wooden point
of my mailbox
makes me smile–
flitting up and down
on the point
at attention–
flitting away
into the day
spring has made.
flitting back
fluttering to attention.

pecking now and
then looking up
soon moving
to the wire above

not going higher
then flying back
to stand sentinel
again, in-borne, well-born,
all creatures serving
destinies for the day.

in winter, no flitting
happens daily
if at all
for elsewhere offers
destinations
for flying, for invitations
in the sun.

Roger Bailey
April 2019

Music and the Early Days...
by Roger D. Bailey

When was the last time
You got up before the sun
And watched while the night and day
Melted into one?

When was the last time
You really looked at rain
Dripping down the gutter
Splashing on the window-pane?

My fondest memories
Are tied around those things
Sunday school, bedtime rules
Grandma's rocking chair

Back in the country
Now I know you're gonna say
Back in the country
Don't you wish that you had stayed?

Back in the country
Where the roses still grow wild
Back in the country
Where you walked those country miles

When was the last time
You saw sundown through a tree
Sitting on the front porch
In a cool evenin' breeze?

When was the last time
That you heard a bobwhite song?
When was the last time?
I'll bet it's been too long

Ada, West Virginia still exists in 2016. I thought it had probably disappeared decades ago. I do have photos of Ada Hollow where my mother says my brothers were born. Their birth certificates say Princeton. She designated such on the backs of several Kodak pictures. I also have another of myself at three, sitting with a birthday cake on a little table in the front yard of the old Ada house. My birth certificate says that Bluefield is my place of birth. I really don't know this beyond the shadow of a doubt. I want to believe that all of "us boys" were born at home, delivered by a roaming Dr. Horton. As my Uncle Lake would say, "Anyhoo, it don't matter." I do know Appalachian fiddle music can take me back to a sense of "belonging" to that area. I feel the comfort as I drive north on Interstate 77 and cross the Virginia state line into the Mountain State of my youth. My few adult visits to this countryside have always resonated with a heart-felt comfort. "I can feel it in my bones," as they say.

Years ago, Mother pointed Dr. Horton out to me in the background of a Kodak photo from the 1930s. She had said that he whistled the same tune a lot. He was a doctor whose rural patients would have required him to travel the roads of West Virginia and Virginia at least from 1927 until 1944, the Bailey boys' birth years. Was he connected with a local hospital? I suppose, but I don't know. I came into this world in February of 1944, eleven years after Bud, my brother nearest in age. So, Dr. Horton, perhaps in various capacities beyond delivering babies, took care of us—the four of us? The five of us?—for twenty years? I don't know. I don't recall my father ever going to a doctor. I'm certain this probably helped him to a stroke in his late fifties. Dr. Horton must've traveled all sorts of twisty mountain roads to get to those who needed him. How was he around enough so that Mother could comment so knowingly about his whistling? I didn't ask questions as I grew into manhood. I just didn't.

Throughout my life I failed to engage my mother in conversations about family. I also recall that my father and I never had an actual conversation at any point. People just didn't talk about personal things much at all. Appalachian, closed-mouthed stoicism, a cultural necessity for lives challenged by hardships. As a balm, my parents did, however, find emotional sustenance and joy in music and, as well, music takes me back to those family gatherings where the radio played in the background. I feel the past in songs that transport me to a porch, a fiddler in the yard, a room, a teary-eyed face, a tapping foot.

Anyway, Dr. Horton's whistling might have been that sort of mindless tune inspired by no musical memory or actual song at all. My mother in later years hummed and whistled as she sat absently curling a lock of hair around her index finger. Dr. Horton surely must have listened to the radio stations in Bluefield, Princeton or maybe even Ada. I remember that we listened to the radio a lot in the late forties and early fifties, slapping our thighs, stomping our feet. Country music and hymns filled the house as we sat through evenings after supper. My father would look up into the air after taking a drag off a cigarette, transported by Little Jimmy Dickens or Roy Acuff or Minnie Pearl. Mother also listened through the week to mountain gospel such as "Blessed Assurance," "Old Time Religion," "Softly and Tenderly," "Rock of Ages," and "In the Garden."

In 1948-49, we moved north along the Big Sandy River to the metropolitan area of Ashland, Kentucky and

Huntington, West Virginia. We had an RCA television set there, which pushed radio from the center of family life and introduced us to theme songs and commercial ditties. Mother, however, never abandoned her sacred mountain tunes and her love of Roy Acuff 's "Back in the Country." Since my retirement from professional life in 2007, the radio has resumed some of its former primacy for me because of National Public Radio's appearance in 1970.

I grew up in the Milton Berle fifties. Theme songs can still rattle through my head: *The Show of Shows,* Loretta Young opening her door, *I Love Lucy,* catchy numbers beginning so many Western serials. Christmas carols, matinee idols and rock and roll came to shape my world as TV and movies grew to entertain (or anaesthetize) America in the years following World War II and the Korean War. Bing Crosby's "White Christmas," Doris Day's "Que Sera Sera" and "Sentimental Journey," Elvis Presley's "Love Me Tender" and "Hound Dog"—well, the number of songs on my LPs and 45s was quite daunting. My adolescence, which was awash in an accelerating musical world, occasionally reemerges for me in 2020 as I slip a memory onto the turntable.

Roger Bailey

4 Prisons in 5+ Years:
Surviving to Move On to a Life of Value Once Again
by Robert Alan Black, PhD

On October 23rd I didn't go to sleep

On October 28th I woke up on the floor of Cell 14

On November 20th I woke up in my own bed at home and many days since

Today I have woken up in my own bed for 18 months

What do these all have in common?

In each case I was waking up in a different prison.

On the 28th of October in 2014 I woke up in Al Wathba Prison, where I was held until November 17th when I was taken to the Superior Court in Abu Dhabi where the three superior judges twice listened to the lawyer who was hired for me by members of the FREE RAB Team to defend me twice that day. That afternoon they ruled NOT GUILTY NO WILFUL INTENT TO DO HARM and ordered that I be released after being at Kalifa Jail and in prison at Al Wathba prison for four+ weeks.

On November 20th, 2014 I woke up in my own bed at home in Athens after having traveled to nine countries since I left in August. During the next few weeks and months I didn't feel I was in prison, until sometime during the next five years I realized I had been in a different prison, but still a prison. A prison where I was no longer hired to do the work I had been doing since 1980 as a speaker, trainer, college professor, or a business consultant who had worked in over 40 US states, Canada and 92 other countries around the globe.

Today I also woke up in my own bed at my home of 34 years in Athens, Georgia. Yet I am still in a prison, though a different one – caused by the current Pandemic that limits where I can go and what I can do every day.

My first jail and prison experience was a personal and professional one that stole four+ weeks of my life and canceled two programs I was scheduled to do for DELL Computer in Malaysia. Thanks to Ms. Chiew Ang they were rescheduled to January 2015.

My days at Kalifa Jail and Al Wathba Prison were very controlled and mostly identical. I received three meals each day that were predictable. I was led out of Cell Block 3 twice each day to go to the clinic to take my various medicines. Tuesdays they opened the store inside the Cell Block so that we could purchase drinks, snacks or clothing items. Wednesday we were allowed to go to the gymnasium for a couple of hours of recreation or to go to the visitor center to meet people. In my case my visitors were pairs of employees from the US Embassy who usually brought copies of faxes they had received from some of my friends or family members: my daughter and her two sons. Each day otherwise was the same. What made the days unique were the different prisoners I would stop and talk with as I walked around and around the Cell Block walkway from when I woke up until I finally lay down to sleep or nap on my bunk in Cell 14.

My professional prison for the last five years didn't become obvious until my work ended, as well as my planned international trips to work with clients and to present at creativity conferences in different countries.

How was that prison different?

I could choose my own food from grocery stores of my choosing or restaurants of my choosing.

How was that prison the same?

No work?

Limited contact with people face to face. Actually I had more of that at Kalifa Jail and Al Wathba Prison.

In the prison there was a television that could be watched.

In my professional prison at home I could watch any of my videos, DVDs or channels I could reach using Netflix basic or Roku.

My most recent prison caused by the Corona or Covid-19 Pandemic is similar to characteristics of the other two but is not identical.

Food? I can buy what I want and eat it when I want. I can order takeout but cannot eat inside a restaurant.

In Al Wathba I could only eat when they let us out three times a day to go to the canteen on the lowest level of the prison building.

I take my medicines twice a day but I choose when I do that.

I can go for walks but feel restricted by the governor's rules and the negative looks of mask-wearing people.

I keep the six-feet distance wherever I go but still do not wear a mask because with my cleft palate and deviated septum I don't think I could breathe easily.

I will if it is made absolutely necessary at Publix, Wal-Mart or the post office.

Entertainment? I have my Netflix, Roku accounts and hundreds of DVDs and videotapes to choose from and my thousands of books.

I read books in Al Wathba.

I read emails throughout every day at home but have rarely completely read any books the past five years.

Because my income is limited I have stopped spending money on books.

In Al Wathba there was a library but I was never able to go due to the visitations of the Embassy people. There was a fellow prisoner who was the Cell Block 3 librarian. I did meet him and he did find a few books in English I could take back to Cell 14 to read.

The Pandemic has closed all bookstores and our libraries.

I do have access to millions of things to read on the www or ebooks through Kindle, and many are free.

Being in prison is a metaphor, a chosen state of mind.

Throughout the last 42 years I have learned to use three techniques to stop my life feeling limited.

Whenever anything bad happens I ask one question:

Will I laugh about this in the future?

Then I find the funny or create it.

I also ask every time:

What's good about it?

— until I can generate a list of at least 12 different benefits or positives.

Also I examine my metaphors and change them to re-create a positive mindset.

Have I really been in prison all these times since October 21st, 2014?

when I was told to stand up

handcuffs were clicked onto my wrists

shackles were clicked onto my ankles

and a solid black hood was pulled down over my head.

Then I accepted I was in trouble on October 21st.

Robert Alan Black, PhD

Cars
by Susan Brassard

When I look at the picture of my four-year-old self next to my parents' new 1948 Plymouth sedan, it reminds me of what that car meant to the family.

It meant freedom. All through WWII my parents did not have a car, making them always live close enough for Dad to walk to work and Mom to be near a neighborhood grocery store. For other activities depending on others was the norm.

As a result of the new car we could now go on vacations or visit family in another town. That first summer we had the car, a camping trip at Wilmington Notch near White Face Mountain in the Adirondacks was on our agenda.

My father somehow rigged the seats so they would be flat. With some padding and several blankets we were able to sleep in the car. Three peas in a pod. This allowed us to have a safe, dry place to sleep while enjoying fishing and other outdoor activities.

As time went on my father would buy a new car every two years, especially after he obtained the job at the Club and his car was considered a write-off. As new cars were purchased my mother, who did not drive, got to choose the color and my father always chose the make. The color was always a surprise but the make was not as it was always a Plymouth.

I was never interested in any of these cars until 1960 when I was able to get my driving permit. Since I had a January birthday, my father made me wait until the New York winter weather cleared enough to make driving safe.

As soon as possible, probably at least March, we were off and I was driving a 1959 Plymouth station wagon. According to Wikipedia the first station wagons were built around 1910, by independent manufacturers producing wooden custom bodies for the Ford Model T chassis. They were originally called "depot hacks" because they worked around train depots and transported people and goods from station to station. It was not a small car. In fact the 1959 Plymouth wagon was one of the largest cars on the market but it had power everything including steering.

Regarding power steering, this is a quote from the 1959 sales brochure.

"By doing most of the work of steering, it relieves driving tensions on long trips and in heavy downtown traffic and enables even the frailest women to park with ease."

The car was a dream to drive as it floated along the road. Driving was addicting, making me always wanting to be in the car – in the driver's seat. I practiced and practiced because my dad wanted me to have my license. By the end of April a license was mine. This meant the summer of 1960 I would be free to go to my girlfriends', shop, and visit family. I was an adult and Dad didn't have to transport me because he was busy at work.

In the fall of 1962 I was off to college and there were no cars in my future. Having a car in college was not a necessity and actually life was easier without one.

Then in August 1965 I married Bill and suddenly I needed a car if we wanted to see each other. I was in Plattsburgh, New York and he lived in Glen Lake, New York, approximately one hundred miles south. He had a job so I needed a car to travel back and forth on the weekends. So at this point I took over the 1959 Chevy convertible. It was quite the hit on campus as it made a great truck but with style. When someone on campus needed furniture or part of a float for Homecoming moved, that car was the ticket. Put the top down, two or three people knelt on the back seat and you could hang onto whatever needed moving. I just made sure I drove slowly through town.

There was only one big issue with the Chevy. If you turned it off, you shouldn't try to restart it when it was hot. I was very careful about remembering that issue as I didn't want to get caught somewhere on campus when I need to be elsewhere.

One Friday as I was heading down Route 9 from Plattsburgh to Glen Lake I decided I would stop at Grand

Union and get some groceries for Bill and me to have dinner. After I turned off the car, my body sank. I realized what I had done.

I found my groceries and paid, at which point I began talking to some guys at the front of the store and told them what had happened. Their answer was, "Don't worry, we'll take care of you." Out of the store we went. They got into their truck and I got into the Chevy. They told me to put my window down so I could hear them yell directions. "Put it in neutral. Okay, here we go!" And they started to push me toward Route 9. Once I was on Route 9 the road went downhill. As I headed downhill I heard them yell, "Crank her up!" I did, and the engine was running. My arm went out the window to wave a thank-you and they beeped their horn. Off I went, never to see them again but so grateful for their help. Soon after that Bill and I decided to spend the wedding money we received and purchase a new car. We bought a 1966 Plymouth Valiant, not as exciting as some of the others. That car is a whole different story.

The last car that was a joy to ride in and to drive was purchased in Hollywood, Florida. We were on our way home from Hollywood Beach and saw it at the Mercury dealership on Sheridan Street. It was a 1969 Mercury

Colony Park station wagon. A car that was smooth and big, with power everything including a freezing A/C and radio better than most stereos of the time. It was 1973 and we would soon be heading to New York to visit family for a month-long trip.

When we headed out on the trip in July, all of our belongings – suitcases, playpen, case of Prosobee and whatever else we needed – were stacked on top of the car, tied down very securely.

That meant we could put the back seat down and cover it with a few comforters, making a huge play and sleeping area for our one- and three-year-olds. Depending upon who was driving Bill and I even used the back area for a nap. So that was how we traveled from Hollywood, Florida to northern New York and Canada and back to Florida.

Then in October 1973 and lasting until March 1974 the oil embargo was in effect, making it quite the problem to get gas if there was any to be sold. I sat in many a line trying to get enough gas to fill up the Mercury's large tank. Most of the time I was limited to ten gallons, which was only a drop for that car. I hardly used the car – only to purchase groceries and transport Scott to preschool because it only got ten miles to a gallon and I had to stretch those gallons.

So our love affair with cars with charm and character had to end. Suddenly we were all about smaller cars that were fuel-efficient. Times changed and so did we. The cars we had in the future were nothing like those of the past. They were small and boxy but fuel-efficient, which is where the world was headed.

I truly loved driving those old cars that floated down the highway leaving you feeling as if you were flying low and all was right with the world. It was hard to let those days go, but the future left us no choice.

Susan Brassard

I Married a Model
by Connie Crawley

I am married to a former model. Yes, I have a trophy husband. Art began modeling when he was a graduate student at Wake Forest University to earn some extra spending money. When he returned home to Louisville, Kentucky, he decided to continue modeling even though he had more than a full-time job at Spalding College managing the student center, running the athletic program, and being the student activities director. Somehow Art always found time to take different modeling jobs despite his busy schedule.

Art was never a supermodel but he was pretty successful in the Kentuckiana area. He has always had a winning smile with nearly perfect teeth that photographed well. He was also blessed with skin that tanned easily and anyone's hair can be enhanced for the camera with a little Summer Blonde. He wore the clothes well because he had big shoulders and narrow hips.

Art did all kinds of modeling in the Louisville area. He would be on the front page of newspaper inserts for the Father's Day sales at the local department stores. He would do runway work at fashion shows at Louisville hotels. He was featured in brochures for new apartment complexes and in newspaper ads for banks. He showed clothes at restaurants while people were lunching – as you may know, Art can talk to anyone anywhere. He even did two commercials: one while driving a dune buggy over the dunes of southern Indiana for Shoney's and another for a Louisville optical company. The optical company even had huge posters of Art in various types of eyewear in each of their stores.

Art even had a wedding picture with a dark-haired bride cutting a wedding cake for an ad for a bridal salon. He always reassured me that he didn't even remember the bride's name.

Probably the most unique job he had occurred early in his career when he was working at the High Point, North Carolina furniture mart. He was asked to wear a giant Naugahyde Man suit. You remember Naugahyde – it was that synthetic leather that was used for lounge chairs in the '60s and '70s. The mascot of the brand was a fake animal that was supposed to be the source of the Naugahyde. Art was so good at playing the part that he was photographed for the newspaper dancing on the streets of High Point. For years, he had two small stuffed Naugahyde Men that he got as part of his compensation for that job.

We really knew Art had made it when Sister Eileen Egan, the president of Spalding College where he worked, put Art's pictures from a catalogue onto the bulletin board outside her office. It was a series of photos from the Stewart's Department Store catalogue with Art modeling pajamas and men's underwear. Let's just say Art was not especially thrilled with that recognition.

While ostensibly Art was modeling for the extra income, he really never made much money. It took gas money to get to the different locations, and most of all, every time he modeled some new outfit he would want to buy it! I think he finally ended his career when he realized that he was in the hole from these jobs and not getting rich.

I started dating Art while he was at the peak of his modeling career. Let's just say I was as un-modelly as anyone could get. I was 21 years old, an undergraduate student, totally makeup-free and not into fashion at all. My typical outfit was a pair of jeans, a turtleneck shirt, a shapeless sweater and tennis shoes. I could dress up, but in contrast to Art, I always looked lost in my clothes.

Whenever I would accompany Art to a social event, and he would introduce me to his friends or acquaintances as his girlfriend, within 10 minutes of talking to me, a new person would ask with a quizzical look, "And how did you two meet?" Yes, I knew we were the odd couple, and I would laugh and explain that we had met at activities he had arranged at my college and we just fell into dating because we had so much in common. For some reason, my looks did not matter to Art. He was more impressed by our common interests.

Also I think I had another unusual trait. I did not waste food! I could eat as much as he could and I never gained an ounce. He had once dated a former Miss Louisville and taken her out for a big steak dinner. She of course only took a few bites because she was probably watching her weight. Not eating the food on one's plate is a MORTAL SIN in Art's book. He just took her steak and put it on his plate and ate both his and hers, and that was the end of their relationship. As they say, beauty is in the eye of the beholder.

There was one issue that did concern Art when we got married. When I was younger, I was SO un-photogenic! I was an an only child, and my mother had taken hundreds of pictures of me with a camera that had a flash bulb that literally blinded me each time she used it. I was like Pavlov's dog anytime a camera appeared, even years later. My eyes would start to water and I would contort my face into the weirdest expressions. Having crooked teeth and acne during my formative years also did not help my confidence in front of the camera. My mother and Art were terrified I would mess up the wedding pictures. But somehow that day I relaxed, or maybe I was just too dazed to be uptight, and the pictures turned out fine. Maybe for one day, the modeling gods took pity on me and made me photogenic for a few hours.

Art's modeling days are long gone. He is still pretty photogenic and probably would still like to pose if given the opportunity, but there are not many jobs for bearded 72-year-olds. Fortunately, I have also overcome my fear of the camera, so we usually have some good pictures together even 43 years after that fateful wedding day.

Connie Crawley

The Beak Girl
by Connie Crawley

When I was 11 years old, my parents and I moved to Louisville, KY. This was pretty traumatic for all of us. We had lived in our hometown, Urbana, OH, all of our lives with an extensive extended family (literally over 30 relatives by marriage or blood within a three-block area). I had even attended the same elementary school since first grade that my father and his parents had attended. What made it worse was that we were moving the day after Thanksgiving instead of at the start of the school year, so I was really going to be at a disadvantage.

In Urbana, I had been close friends with what I considered the "popular girls." We were the ones who got chosen for the school plays, competed with each other for the best grades and played at each other's homes on a weekly basis – enjoying sleepovers and parties. I never doubted my position in the classroom or on the social ladder.

Walking into my new classroom, I could tell things were going to be different. While my friends in Ohio were all about my height and weight, in this new classroom I was much taller and bigger than most of the 6th-grade students. All my flaws that were overlooked by my friends in Urbana suddenly set me apart in this new environment: eyeglasses, acne, and teeth that needed braces.

Fairly quickly the pecking order became obvious to me. The girls on the swim team at the local country club were the "in" girls and I was not one of them. The two ringleaders were Paula and her best friend, Debra, and they quickly decided to put me in my place. They plopped themselves down next to me at the lunch table one day and told me that they didn't like girls with red hair. I had never been told I had red hair, since I had always been considered a strawberry blond, so I calmly told them I did not have red hair. They quickly amended their condemnation to not liking girls with dirty blond hair (which, by the way, they both had). I just stared at them with contempt.

That was just the beginning of my interaction with these two, especially with Paula. She was the type of girl who loved to get attention any way she could, whether it was tormenting other kids or jumping feet first into the new trash can in the girl's restroom. For the two remaining years of elementary school, she probably did not do more to me than anyone else she singled out, but it was the anticipation of what she could do that added dread to my days. I never knew when she would direct her attention my way and add to my adolescent humiliation.

I called her the Beak Girl because she had a nose that looked like an owl's beak to me, especially since she wore big round blue glasses. I related so many stories about her escapades at school to my parents that eventually my father began to ask each night at supper, "What did the Beak Girl do today?"

Unfortunately Paula followed me to high school and she was placed in my Latin class. In our new school, her status seriously fell, so she seemed to need to torment me even more so she could feel better about herself. Of course she chose to sit directly behind me in class and each day she would try to do something to aggravate me such as shoving my books off my desk, stealing my pencil, pulling at my shirt collar or tugging my hair. Anything to get my goat. I was sitting directly in front of our teacher, Sister Bernard, so I tried to stay composed.

Sister Bernard was probably close to 80 at this time, and when she sat down at her desk all you saw was her head and the top part of her veil, but she didn't miss much. I am sure she was very aware of Paula's treatment of me, but I never remember her telling Paula to stop.

Finally one day I had had enough. When Paula started picking at my shirt and hair, I just turned around without thinking and slapped her as hard as I could across the face in front of the whole class and Sister Bernard. Of course Paula ducked, and the slap was not as effective as it could have been, but I had finally gotten my revenge.

Of course the minute I turned back around, there sat Sister Bernard staring at me. I could feel my face turning red with embarrassment, and I expected punishment at any moment, but Sister Bernard just looked calmly at me and then said to Paula, "You deserved that," and promptly went on with class. To say I felt vindicated that day would be to put it mildly.

I cannot say that Paula never tried to bully me again. She followed me into German class, as well as Latin class, the next year and remained in German class with me until we both graduated, but I think she knew that she'd better not bother me too much. She still managed to sit behind or beside me in class and occasionally would try something, but I learned to just give her the evil eye, and I never ever had to get physical with her again.

Connie Crawley

Milo
By Peggy Harrington

Yesterday Jim and I surrendered Milo to the animal rescue (ARF) in East Hampton. His black fur gleamed as we turned him over to the director. I noticed that Jim's eyes were watery. When I mentioned it, he said that he had just sneezed. Then my eyes misted over. We both love Milo and had great fun with him over the months that he was with us. He was just too much dog. When we adopted him, I thought that with the proper training he could be controlled. We rescued him last September when he was three months old. He was listed as a German shepherd mix, which he isn't. It turns out that he is a Labrador retriever mix. Since he has ticking under his jaw and down his chest, there is a limited number of breeds that he could be. The ticking looks like black-and-white tweed. Only certain breeds have that marking. German shorthaired pointers (GSP) and Great Danes are two of them. I thought from the beginning that he was part GSP. When we first adopted Milo, in an attempt to find his mix, I went online and pulled up pictures of the various breeds that have ticking. The pictures of GSP puppies at three to four months old looked very much like him. There were other possibilities. Four different veterinarians conjectured that he could be part Great Dane. I wasn't sure about that. His paws were big, but not that big. I stuck to the Labrador retriever and GSP options. Some people suggested that we have DNA testing.

I laughed thinking that wolf would certainly be found in his ancestry. When we turned him in at ARF, the director mentioned that she thought he was part GSP without any prompting from me. She also mentioned that the pointer is a rambunctious breed. Go, Milo!

Milo got too big for us to control. He weighs over sixty pounds. And he is rambunctious. At times he would go wild, more like crazy wild, where he would lunge at us and nip and bite. He did this in play, but we had trouble stopping him. Jim's skin is thin, since he takes a low dose of aspirin. One time he fell, and while he was trying to get up, Milo jumped all over him. When I looked out from the porch, I saw Jim struggling to get up. I could see that his arm was bleeding. As I went down to the yard, I yelled at Milo to stop. Milo looked up and froze. I have to say that except for those crazy times, Milo was a sweet-tempered dog. Really. He is very smart. He learned all the commands that a puppy should know: *Sit, Down, Stay, Come, Leave it.* He loved dried grass and the wood chips from the recent stump removal in our yard.

Milo had gained our trust. He learned well what he could touch and not touch inside the house. He joined Jim on the porch and watched television with us sometimes at night. I learned to love our backyard in the early hours of the morning and in all kinds of weather. I re-familiarized myself with birdcalls and spring flowers. I began to learn the habits of some of our neighbors. One car from the house next door left at 7:45 every weekday morning. A student from down the street roared past our house on his motorcycle at 8:45. Dog owners are always up and out early. I met Bill with tiny Sophia, who was part of a study on the effects of service dogs on students with autism. I met George walking his dog who resembled Milo. She was older, blind, and deaf.

Jim and I took Milo to puppy training for eight weeks at the local pet store, and he was awarded a certificate of completion. We continued his training in a group situation, with a plan developed by the American Kennel Club. We also hired a trainer who came to the house. She taught us some really good commands. "Focus" and "Touch" came in handy. We used "Focus" when Milo sat on command. Looking at Milo, we would say, "Focus," and then wait for him to lock eyes with us. This was a powerful way to gain his attention and establish who was in control. After he locked eyes with us, he'd get a treat. The other command, "Touch," was for when we had him on the leash for a walk. I put treats in my hand on the side where he was walking. As we walked, with a treat in my hand, I would put my hand on the top of his nose and say, "Touch." With this command I could get him to walk by my side. I let him have the treat periodically as we walked along. Also, if he was pulling on the leash, I could stop and say, "Touch," guiding him back to my side with a sweeping arm gesture. When he returned to my side, I gave him the treat. He was quite motivated by food.

The biggest problem was that he didn't learn to walk without pulling. Also, he continued to jump and lunge at us when he went puppy crazy. But then he got to be over sixty pounds. Ouch. Other than that, he was good company. He was smart and fun. He was addicted to playing ball. He even made up his own games and had a sense of fair play.

For the last two weeks we kept Milo in day care because he wasn't able to run around the yard. There were wood chips that were waiting to be removed and he would make a meal of them if we let him loose. He loved going to day care. On the second day of the first week, when Jim stopped in front of the building, Milo jumped out of the back of the car and ran to the door to the facility. A week before that, when he stayed overnight, he fell into the day care's outdoor pool. After that, he wanted to play fetch in the water. I wish I could have seen that. What fun that must have been! I was pleased that he enjoyed the pool, because in the winter he shunned the heated indoor pool and after all, he is part Labrador. His feet are webbed. He was made for water. Marco Polo, anyone?

There were lots of dogs barking while I filled out the forms for Milo's surrender. I hope they let the dogs out to run. Milo needs to exercise on a regular basis. I was told that he would be evaluated for five days and then his photo would go up on the adoption website.

Jim and I hope that Milo will be rescued quickly.

Auf Wiedersehen, Milo.

Peggy Harrington
June 1, 2020

Untitled
By Richard Horner

Memoir writing can take many forms: recitation of a life's events, detailed review of specific events, description of the forces that shaped a life, or even autobiography masquerading as fiction. For someone who has lived a long time, succeeded at some things, failed at others, one form of memoir that could be useful is to ask what I have learned so far. To ask this question, I have shamelessly hijacked a device from the TV series *Bluebloods*: what advice would I give my younger self? It's artificial, in a way a straw man, but it has its uses. With that said, here is some advice to my younger self: (l) Be more curious; dig deeper into the experience and thoughts of those close to you, and of some of those not as close to you. Their insights and memories and knowledge can be interesting and valuable and may not be available forever. (2) Use your imagination more. Spend more time in the shoes of others, thinking about why they feel the way they feel and do what they do and what they might need. (3) Let "it" happen instead of trying to make "it" happen; "it" might be love, or deciding what work to do or how to spend your life or where to live or how to succeed in your career. This is not to advise passivity but rather to attend to what you are experiencing, to what your intuition tells you, and to understand the difference between how things are versus how they "should" be. (4) Think honestly and carefully about your failures in all the arenas of your life. You've contributed mightily to most of them; understanding why and how they happened can prevent repetition. (5) Every month, every six months, every year, however often, climb out of the forest to the top of the mountain to see where you are, where you've been and where you might need or want to go. It's too easy to get used to the worm's-eye view.

Younger self, this advice isn't comprehensive, but maybe it can be useful…even to my older self.

Richard J. Horner
November 2019

Holes in the Yard
By Sharon Hughes

I've lived in old houses, so I know about mice. Sneaky little rodents who make nests in your bedroom closet, and eat cereal in the pantry.

I've lived in a pecan grove, so I've dealt with pesky squirrels who gnaw metal clips that hold up gutters, and make their nests in the attic.

But, today I met a critter I never, ever, expected to see in my yard, right here in Athens, Georgia.

> I noticed the first holes
> Right beside my deck
> I thought a wayward squirrel
> Was making little pecks
>
> As days went by more holes appeared
> On each side of our house
> What made these holes
> I really feared, was larger than a mouse
>
> John called me out to look at more
> What he told me made me bellow
> Oh no! Dear me! How could it be?
> Invaded by armadillos!

They're supposed to be in Texas
It's really more their style
But they've been creeping Eastward now
For quite a little while

I read my class "Armadillo Rodeo"
We learned they are quite blind
Just perhaps the dastardly things
Couldn't read road signs!

Sharon Hughes

The Dirt Tracks of New York State
By Sharon Hughes

My Dad loved cars. He loved driving them. He loved working on them. He loved racing them.

The first car I remember, vaguely, mostly from family stories, was a worn-out DeSoto that transported us back and forth from our apartment in Newburgh, N.Y., to the little house Daddy was building in the midst of dairy farms in nearby New Windsor. The poor old car had no back seat, and no real front seat. It had only a seat for the driver, and a wooden crate that my Mom straddled, with me in her lap. We held on tightly while Daddy maneuvered the car over narrow, bumpy dirt roads.

Not long after we moved into our tiny new home, on Halloween night, 1951, Daddy started creating his dream car – a stock car for the many dirt racetracks of the day. He was going to be a race car driver! I don't know where the car came from, or what kind it was, but I do know, as soon as the little coupe showed up in our back yard, so did my dad's many racing friends. They all wanted to be a part of Daddy's pit crew. It was all very curious and exciting to a small girl. The men showed up each night after dinner, and I would hear their voices outside my bedroom window, long after I was put to bed. Weekends were full of the sounds of banging tools on metal, and eventually, the revving of the engine. At long last it was time for the finishing touches. The body was painted burgundy and white. Three large number ones were painted on each door. The number one-eleven was ready to go!

We became a race track family. Every Saturday we loaded up the car on a trailer, and towed it to one of the many dirt tracks nearby. We would eat meatball subs, or pizza, and drink Cokes. I played with the other race car kids under the bleachers. When the races began we would run to our moms and cheer on our dads, to the roars of the engines as they made their way around the small, quarter-mile tracks. Dirt flew. Emotions were high. Every driver had their eye on that checkered flag. I don't remember if Daddy ever even won a race, but I do know we were always happy, tired, and filthy dirty on the drive home. And I always knew on Monday Daddy's pit crew would be back to fix what was broken, and start all over to get ready for the next week's race.

Sitting on Dad's 111

In 1954 Dad had to tighten his belt, because there would be a new mouth to feed in October. No more money to pour into an old beat-up race car. But when my brother

Gary arrived, Dad had met his best car-loving buddy. His first words were "car" and "truck."

Uncle Gary's coupe

By the time he was three, he could identify every make of car while we drove around town. When my dad built a garage so he could work on cars at home, Gary was always nearby, soaking up everything there was to know about fixing a car. Eventually a friend built a stock car in Dad's garage, and I went to sleep to the sounds of a pit crew again.

We went to the races every Saturday night. The Middletown Speedway was a wonderful place. It was the site of the Orange County Fair each August, and Fair Week was my absolute favorite week of the summer racing season. Added to the excitement of the race, we could hear the music and laughter of the fair, mixed with the luscious aromas of fair food behind our seats in the bleachers.

As years went by, I married, and moved to Georgia. But we traveled to New York every summer. And on Saturday nights we introduced racing to our three children.

My brother, Gary, went to vocational school and learned the art of Auto Body Work. He and Dad built

Deckers Garage in the back yard. And it was no surprise when Gary built his own race car in the early 1970s. It was another little coupe. It was burgundy and white. But this number was one-o-one.

The newest 101

My children gravitated toward the garage on our visits, eyes wide, listening to the men as they worked on Gary's car. The sounds of mallets striking metal, the sputtering of the engine as it came to life, and the random Spit! Splat! of Daddy's Red Man chewing tobacco hitting the floor, filled the air.

Cars were faster now. The excitement was the same. Saturday nights meant the racetrack to my children when we were at Grandma and Grandpa's. We all watched Gary roar around the track just like Daddy had.

We gasped at the near misses, cars slamming into the walls, or into each other. Even flying through the air! All in the quest for that checkered flag.

And each time, my three children had the same happy, filthy faces on the ride home that I did when I was a little girl.

Yes, my Daddy loved cars. And he and Gary spent their lives together, driving them, fixing them, and racing them. They're both gone now. But sometimes we will see the number 101 on a license plate, or smell fair food, or hear the sounds of cheering crowds, and our minds are transported back to those happy, exciting, thrill-filled nights at the dirt tracks of New York State.

Sharon Hughes

The last check before the race

I Finally Got My Nickel
By Linda Jones Jenkins

My first-grade teacher, Mae Jones, and my father were first cousins. Mae's father, Uncle Beryl, and my father's mother, Annie, were brother and sister and had always enjoyed close family relationships with their three brothers and their families. As we all know, there are frequently incidents that impact those familial bonds that eventually come into the light, and this one is no exception. Only as adults would we Jones children learn why Cousin Mae and Uncle Beryl never came to visit my parents during the 14 years we lived in Stockton, MD on the Eastern Shore of Maryland, although only two miles separated our houses.

My father's grandfather, Alma Thomas Jones, was born in 1852 and married Elizabeth Ann Payne in 1874. About a year afterward, my great-grandparents, Pop Pop Al and Grandma Liz, bought a farm two miles from Stockton and set up housekeeping in an antebellum "telescope" house where they would raise one daughter, Annie, my father's mother, along with four sons, one of whom was Uncle Beryl. By 1906 their four sons were grown and had

Alma Thomas Jones
May 11, 1852 –
April 11, 1927

left home, taking their free farm-labor with them. Al and Liz sold their farm to retire to a less active life in nearby Pocomoke City. Beryl and Annie were the only two of their children who remained in close proximity, often lending a hand to help their parents and each other. Al and Liz would have nine years to enjoy the fruits of their labor and town-life when Grandma Liz suddenly died in 1915, at the young age of 60. Some say she never recovered from the shock of the accidental death of her youngest son, John, three years earlier.

Pop Pop Al, unsuited to the solitary life, sold the family home in Pocomoke and took his life's savings to Wilmington, DE where he found work as an elevator operator. He did not, however, find love, which is likely what he was looking for. Word has it that he looked in all the wrong places. My father's account was that his grandfather was fleeced by a certain femme fatale. In a couple of years, having gone through his retirement funds, he returned to the Shore seeking refuge for his old age, penniless, a gold watch his only possession. Pop Pop Al, known to be a cantankerous man, was not easy to live with. After his four sons, including Uncle Beryl, denied him a home to live out his remaining years, he appealed to his only daughter, my grandmother Annie. So. Pop Pop Al ended up a "prisoner in Annie's home," as he tells us in an intercepted letter to his son Frank, "sleeping in the coldest room in the house and invited by the family to go nowhere, but to church." He

c. 1923, my father,
George A. Jones, age 13

would live with my dad's family during the final ten years of his "miserable" life.

Being the youngest child in the family, it fell to my father, from ages 6 to 16, to attend to the needs of his grumpy grandfather, who also suffered terribly from rheumatism. Pop Pop Al often asked young George to bring firewood to his second-floor bedroom, and asked him to rub his pain-racked limbs and joints with Sloan's Liniment, promising him a nickel for each rub. For ten years, my dad dutifully ran errands and rubbed Pop Pop Al's back, hands and feet, but, sadly, never saw one buffalo nickel. Toward the end of Al's life, feeling guilty for all the IOUs for ten years of attention, he promised his grandson, my dad, his only valuable possession, his gold watch.

In 1927, when news of Al's death reached Uncle Beryl, he immediately went to help his sister attend to their father's funeral. Later, when my father looked for his gold watch in Al's bedroom, and it was nowhere to be found, it was assumed that Beryl had quietly removed it. Otherwise, we do not know how the watch ended up in Beryl's pocket. Annie knew that the watch had been promised to George. Did Beryl just take it? Did he tell Annie he took it? Did Annie decide to defer to her brother in lieu of her son? After all of that Sloan's Liniment and all of the firewood carted upstairs, and after all those promised nickels that never materialized … how was it possible? … no watch, no nothing! Poor George.

The next time the family gathered to help Uncle Beryl get in his hay, my 16-year-old father got up his nerve and reminded his uncle that Pop Pop Al had promised the gold watch to him and said he would like to take possession of it. Beryl pretended not to hear, launching at once into some unrelated story to cover his tracks, and, in the hustle and bustle of the hay activity, George did not get to renew his suit. He went home without the watch, but with a lifetime of disappointment in his Uncle Beryl.

My dad's mother, not wanting to "upset the apple cart," told him to let it go, but what he let go of was the relationship. Of course, I didn't know anything about this duplicity when I was Mae's student in first and second grades. However, when I was in my 50s, my brother, Bob, asked me if I could remember Uncle Beryl or Cousin Mae ever visiting our house in Stockton. Not one time could I recall, and they lived just two miles away. The only time I visited them at their house, I was with my grandmother or my Aunt Bessie.

Although we Jones children had all been students of Cousin Mae, we only became aware of the gold watch story after my father, at age 78, went to live with my brother in 1992. A couple of years after hearing the story, my brother went to the courthouse to do some research and learned that when Uncle Beryl died in 1963, he left a gold watch to his daughter, Mae. Further, when she died in 1994, she left the watch to Stephen Pryor, her husband's Florida grandson – of no kin whatsoever to Pop Pop Al. However, Mae had stipulated in her will that if Stephen predeceased my brother, Bob, that the watch should go to him.

On the strength of that stipulation, and taking into account the years of faithful service my father had provided to his grandfather, and Pop Pop Al's promise to fulfill his IOU obligation to George, Bob took it upon himself to write to Stephen. He recounted Pop Pop Al's sad story, of all the errands, all the back rubs, and unfulfilled nickel IOUs, and of the promised watch, and, of course, offered to pay for the watch and its return. Several weeks later, a box arrived in the mail from Florida. My brother, upon opening it, reported, "Imagine the thrill of seeing an heirloom of that magnitude and antiquity materialize – an item out of circulation since 1927, that is, 67 years! Yes, you guessed right: Pop Pop Al's gold watch was in the box."

Bob recounts his surprise presentation of the watch to our father: "As Dad sat in the living room that Thanksgiving evening in 1994, with several children and grandchildren present, I never saw a look of such total surprise on my father's face as when he opened that box. Dad explained again how his mother had asked him to refrain from claiming the watch once it was discovered that her brother, Beryl, had removed it from Grandpop Al's room upon his death. Opening the watch case and running his fingers over the gold chain, Dad looked up with an extraordinary and unforgettable grin. 'Well, I guess I finally got my nickel!'"

Linda Jones Jenkins

c. 1911 Grandma Liz (11) and Pop Pop Al (13). My Grandmother Annie (1), her brother, Beryl (5), and my father (10). Mae, Beryl's daughter, my first-grade teacher and Dad's first cousin (12). The gold watch chain is visible in Pop Pop Al's pocket.

Sinking Holiday Spirits
By Terry Kaley

I married Steve Kaley in February 1972. I was 20 years old and he was one week shy of turning 45. It was a first marriage for both of us. They said it would never last. And, in the end, they were right. The following December we had our first Christmas together. Now, I grew up in Texas, and my family always had a big Christmas with a decorated tree, lots of presents, and big family get-togethers. In contrast, Steve grew up in Bremen, GA during the Great Depression. They didn't have much to eat back then. On a normal day they ate biscuits and gravy for breakfast, black-eyed peas for lunch, and a little something with two pieces of bread each for dinner. At Christmas Steve and his brothers would go out into the woods and cut down an evergreen tree and bring it home. They decorated with what few decorations they had, but there were never many presents under the tree. Toys were passed down from one child to the next. However, Steve's father was the railroad stationmaster, and every Christmas he brought home a large burlap sack of oranges that came up from Florida on the train. And Steve's mother would bake six different kinds of cakes. It was the only time of year she baked a cake. Steve was the youngest of six children, and he recalled with delight being able to eat oranges out of the sack or a piece of cake whenever he wanted to. Other than that his family didn't have much of a Christmas.

So, back to Christmas 1972. Steve and I had a major clash of Christmas traditions. I wanted to buy a Christmas tree, and Steve thought that paying $8.00 for a tree was extravagant. I whined and pouted until he mentioned our disagreement to his sister. She told him about some property a friend of hers owned where we could go cut down a tree for free. Well, that sounded good to him. So, on Saturday morning we drove to the wooded property and set off on foot with axe in hand. After hiking a short distance, we came to a sandy place where the ground dropped down a foot or so. Steve stepped down and his right leg sank in up to his hip. Struggle as he might, he couldn't get out. I laughed at him, which made him mad. Finally, I stepped down to help him out, and I sank in up to my knee. I was stuck, and it wasn't funny anymore. Steve was no gentleman. He delighted in my predicament and laughed at me. That made me mad, and I wanted to swing the axe at his head. I felt panicky when I couldn't pull my leg out. "Man, we're in quicksand," I realized. I strained and I struggled, and finally I pulled my leg out of the sand. I managed to claw myself up onto solid ground. Then I extended the axe handle to Steve. He grabbed on and I tugged and I pulled and I cussed. Finally, he popped free from the sand, and I pulled him up onto solid ground. By then we were both caked with wet, gritty sand, so we hiked back to the car. We drove home, stripped down, and put our clothes in the washing machine. We put on warm, clean, dry clothes. Then we went out and bought a Christmas tree!

And, thus was born "our" Christmas tradition. Every year after that we had to do everything exactly the same way, except for getting stuck in quicksand, because Steve would say, "We always do it this way." And, that's what we did for the next 44 years. We liked to collect Christmas tree ornaments everywhere we travelled over those many years.

Each year we'd decorate our tree and enjoy recalling where we were when we got each ornament. Then, at the age of 89 Steve passed away. For the first time in my life I just didn't have the heart to put up a Christmas tree. But, the next year a good friend helped me put up a Christmas tree. Later I decorated it alone and as I hung each ornament I had a happy memory to go with it. Finally, I plugged in the lights and stepped back to look at the decorated tree. And then I thought, "It's beginning to look a lot like Christmas."

Terry Kaley

Mother Buys a House
by Tom Kenyon

During World War II, my mother bought a house! It was the first house my parents owned. She was able to buy it because my Dad had won over $4,000 playing craps. He was in the Navy, a Seabee, stationed on Okinawa in the Pacific. It was against all military rules to gamble, but the sailors did it anyway. Dad had no way of getting the money to my mother. He was not supposed to have it. Dad told us after he got home that he had to carry the money with him at all times, lest it be stolen, which was not an easy task with his duties.

His senior officer received what was called bereavement leave as one of his parents had passed away. It was for two weeks. The officer's family was in Quincy, Illinois, about a hundred miles north of St. Louis. My father went to his officer and asked him if he could deliver a small package to my mother in St. Louis. He said it was very important and would mean the world to his family. My dad said he would pay for his costs. This particular officer knew my dad quite well, as they had been in basic training together, and thought well of him. He said he would do his best but could not promise as he didn't know how things would be with his family. My dad knew the officer knew what was in the package. Military mail censorship being what it was, my dad had not been able to write my mother about any of this.

We lived in a four-family flat. Our unit had a living room, dining room, kitchen, bedroom, bath and screened-in porch. It was on the second floor. When my dad left for the service my mother's best friend, Minette, moved in with us. Minette's husband, Francis, was also in the Navy. Mother and Minette needed to economize. Seaman's pay was $65 a month. Sharing rent meant they could cut their housing costs in half. Two weeks after Minette came to live with us she gave birth to twins, a boy, Bobby, and a girl, Sherie. My sister Joy and I were thrilled at the prospect of babies. Six people, three under the age of two years, in a four-room unit was the furthest thing from our young minds. Sometime after that, a friend of Mother's and Minette's, a woman named Virginia, also moved in with us. Her husband was in the Army. She worked in a war plant for McDonnell Douglas. Virginia slept on the sofa in the living room in the cold months and on the screened-in porch in the warm months.

One day, when mother was alone in the flat the doorbell rang. She looked out the window to see who it was. Her knees felt weak. Her stomach tied in a knot. It was a Navy officer holding a package! She was terrified to answer the door. She remembered thinking how grateful she was that Minette had taken all of us for a walk in Forest Park. When she opened the door the officer asked her if she was Esther Kenyon. She said she was. He handed her the package and said, "Tom asked me to deliver this to you." Mother asked, "What is it?"

"I don't know," the officer said. He suggested she wait to open it until she was upstairs. As he was turning to leave he said, "Write to Tom and tell him his mission was accomplished." — The mission being to get the money to my mother. When she was upstairs she opened the package and saw the money. She was dumbfounded! She counted it out! How did this happen? Where did Dad come by this money? Did he do something terrible? Why did a Navy officer deliver it if there was something wrong?

When we children and Minette came back from our walk, Mother helped her get us upstairs. The twins and Joy were put down for their naps. Since I was the man of the house my mother told me to sit in my place at the kitchen table. When she handed the package to Minette, she let out a cry of disbelief. "Oh Lord, where, where, where!" she said. Mother told her what had happened moments before. They both cried. They jumped up and down. They hugged each other.

I don't recall how much time passed, but it must have been sooner than later that Mother bought the house at 1208 McCausland Avenue. It was a two-story house three blocks west on McCausland Avenue from the flat and closer to Forest Park. It seemed like a mansion to me. In reality it was probably less than 800 square feet total! There was a large living room, a dining room, and a kitchen on the first floor. Upstairs, there were two large bedrooms and a bath. The backyard was huge in my eyes. It had climbing roses, daylilies, irises, and a persimmon tree. For us four children our living space was tripled!

The night before the move the four of us stayed overnight at my grandparents' house. I was so excited I couldn't sleep. Moving day seemed like an eternity. Finally we drove to our new house. Mother met us at the front door and led Joy and me inside. Minette lifted the twins from their chair seats and carried them in. Grandma and Grandpa followed. The living room had a new sofa and chair. There was a dining room table and china cabinet. The kitchen had a new table and four chairs, plus two high chairs. My parents kept that kitchen set their entire married life. When I was tasked to break up my parents' home it was impossible to dispose of my mother's table. I rented a truck and drove it back to Connecticut and stored it in the barn. Years later when my wife and I were downsizing we invited our nieces and nephews to select what they wanted. My niece wanted the kitchen table and it now is her worktable in Athens, Georgia!

The house was twice as big as our old flat. In one of the bedrooms Mother had her bedroom set. Mother bought me my own single bed! And my own little chest of drawers. I slept on that bed until I left home at 21. I took my little dresser with me. Joy would sleep with Mother. Minette took the other bedroom. After her bedroom furniture and the two cribs were placed you could hardly walk around. Virginia did not make the move. She had found a room with an elderly lady one block away. My grandmother had cooked a meal and brought it with us. Minette's mother took the streetcar and brought a dessert. We all sat down to our first meal at our new dining table! Grandpa said grace and made a little speech. He said we were blessed Tom had found a way to get the money to Mother. Moving day was the happiest day of my young life. Mother had paid $3,500 cash for the house, and $325 for the furniture and put the rest away for a rainy date.

When the war ended, all the children in our neighborhood tied old pots and pans to the back of our bikes, scooters and wagons and rode up and down the street yelling, "The war is over!" Everyone was honking their car horns as they drove by. The fire stations sounded their sirens. Everyone on our block gathered to talk to each other, some for the first time. That night my grandparents came over and we all listened on the radio to President Truman tell us it was VJ Day and that the war with Japan was over. Mother and Minette cried. I had a vague recollection of my dad. I saw his picture but didn't remember much about him. Joy had no recollection of him at all.

Francis came home sometime in late 1945. He moved in with us and shared Minette's room. Dad didn't get home until 1946. Dad had no idea Mother had bought a house. He thought we had moved into another flat down the street on McCausland Avenue. Mother never told him she used the money to buy a house because she was afraid the Navy would come and want the money back. Dad flew into Lambert Field in St. Louis from Seattle. We were all waiting to greet him: Francis and Minette and the twins, my grandparents, Mother, Joy and I. As the men came off the plane they were directed to form lines. A senior officer stepped forward to a microphone; we couldn't understand him. He read a letter from President Truman thanking the men and said they were discharged from their Naval service. With that, all pandemonium broke loose. The men ran to the gate and poured through to find their families. When Dad saw us and we ran to him he was so overwhelmed he could not speak. All at once the reality of the war, the separation, his coming home to his wife and children, his best friends, and his parents-in-law left him trembling. He later said he had never had so many hugs and kisses in his life.

Uncle Joe had let Mother use his car so we could come home as a family of four. Grandpa drove his car with everyone else. They took a longer time to get home so we would arrive first. When we pulled up in front of the house, Dad asked, "Why are we here? How much is the rent on this place?"

Mother said, "Don't worry about that now, Tom. Let's go in." The look on his face when he walked in and Mother told him it was their house is something I have never forgotten.

Joy and I were laughing, Dad was hugging Mother and then us. When everyone got to the house we all sat at the dining room table and Dad related to us how he had asked his superior officer to bring Mother the money, and Mother related how she wrote to let Dad know the mission was accomplished. Knowing there would be a housing shortage once the war was over, she was determined to buy a place so we would all be settled when Dad came home.

Within a few months, Francis and Minette and the twins moved into their new house. Joy and I moved into her bedroom. Joy got a new single bed and little dresser.

Oddly, Dad's return was difficult for Joy and me. Who was this man? He didn't seem to know how we had all managed without him. We loved Minette and she loved us. We thought of the twins as our little sister and brother. After they moved away we missed them terribly. Grandpa and Grandma wanted to give Mother and Dad some space, so their visits were less frequent. Grandpa stopped reading us the funny paper over the phone before dinner. I was sent to a Catholic school and hated it. My teacher was a witch in black and she scared me. And worst of all for me, I was no longer the man of the house.

Tom Kenyon

Adopting Kathleen
by Nancy MacNair

(Or Nguyen Thi Hoang Yen, the Vietnamese name she was given by the orphanage, where she was left anonymously on the steps, at birth)

So, why on earth would my husband and I want to adopt a Black/Vietnamese baby girl???

Just because we had already adopted Steven, a Black/white baby boy, and we <u>wanted</u> another child, but didn't want to add to the population. Also, because we had lived in the Black community of Tuskegee Institute, AL, for five years at that time and had a sense of relatedness to Black people and Black culture. In addition, we had lived in India and had relatives who had lived in Thailand, so we felt an Asian connection. We felt that having an interracial, international family would enrich us all. Plus, we had feelings of horror at the whole Viet Nam War. Our Quaker, pacifist backgrounds led us to oppose the war, and to a feeling that we would like to do one small thing to mitigate the tragedy.

So, we applied to Catholic Social Services in Montgomery, AL, who had been very positive and helpful in finding and placing our son, Steven, with us. We had a home study done and were approved. (By that time, American Black or Black/white babies were finally being placed with Black families, under pressure from Black social workers, a good thing.)

After two years of trying to be helpful, both in the US and abroad, Catholic Social Services was unable to find a baby for us. Finally, I was able to contact a group of women in Boulder, CO, who had formed an agency called "Friends of Children of Viet Nam," working out of their kitchens. Their husbands had served as military doctors in Viet Nam, and had visited orphanages, played with the children, and given money for supplies.

I later saw the movie *Green Eyes,* about a Black veteran searching for his Vietnamese baby. There was actual footage, I believe, of hundreds of orphans, just lying on mats on the concrete floors. That film absolutely horrified me. I knew that if Kathleen had stayed in Viet Nam, she would have been subject to extreme prejudice, if she had even managed to stay alive. Such prejudice was directed to <u>any</u> mixed children, but was even worse if they were Black.

The Colorado agency was encouraging, helpful, and prompt, with very clear instructions and fairly low costs. We began the bureaucratic process of adoption, filling out reams of paperwork. We even had to have a letter from the mayor of Tuskegee (a Vietnamese requirement). Luckily, Ray, my husband, had worked to help elect him, the first Black mayor (of a city 95 percent Black).

But now the problems with the state of Alabama began, and took the next six months to be resolved. They objected to the Colorado agency not being licensed, though they were in the process and had successfully placed hundreds of babies in other states already.

Then, they claimed they had to have the Vietnamese mother's signature. But these babies were abandoned anonymously on the steps of orphanages at birth, and numerous other states had accepted the signatures of heads of the orphanages.

They also wanted a copy of Vietnamese adoption law, translated into English, which naturally took a while to procure.

And, they insisted that all communication from Catholic Social Services to the Colorado agency be routed through Alabama state officials, and this prolonged all procedures.

Finally, they warned us that this was a trial situation, and if they granted permission, we should notify our lawyer, in case trouble arose. (Our lawyer was Fred Gray, who had been MLK Jr.'s lawyer in civil rights cases, now practicing in Tuskegee.)

Alabama also refused for six and a half months to release our approved home study, which the Colorado agency had to have before selecting a child for us. Alabama thus delayed from February 18 until September first, when they finally released the home study.

The Colorado doctors' wives acted almost immediately, and we received a photo of a baby, named Nguyen Thi Hoang Yen, born April 14, 1973, now five or six months old, sitting forlornly, propped up on a concrete floor. Meanwhile, she had been lying on her back in the orphanage, and had had pneumonia at age three months, we were told later.

We then had to wait the normal five weeks for immigration and travel procedures. We did not have to travel to Viet Nam (still at war) or pay exorbitant fees. Still, the money, red tape, and little publicity meant that US Black families rarely applied, unfortunately.

After more time passed, and our frazzled nerves were almost worn out, we were finally informed that she would be flown from Viet Nam, arriving at Kennedy Airport, NY, on December 12, 1973.

My parents drove me to the airport, where we waited impatiently for her plane. We were told that there would be eleven babies on board. But when the plane arrived – NO BABIES …

More waiting, until we were eventually told that one of the Catholic Sisters accompanying the babies had had her purse stolen in Saigon, with all her papers in it. Hence, the delay. But we were <u>promised</u> that the babies would be on the next plane, arriving via Paris.

At last, the plane <u>did</u> arrive, and there <u>were</u> babies, who had been just plunked on the laps of regular passengers for the trip! We were told that Kathleen had been sick during the flight, very quiet and sober. The attendants called her "The Little Buddha."

After a flight to Atlanta, met by Ray and our other three children, I placed Kathleen in Ray's arms so I could go to the restroom. As I walked off, I could hear her crying, "Ma, ma, ma …." I could just imagine hundreds of babies in the orphanage crying just that piteously.

When we got home, Ray tried to bounce her on his knees, and her legs just crumpled. She had no strength in them at age eight months, having been lying in that orphanage all that time. Her head was also slightly flattened in back (and still is today), and the hair on the back of her head was partly worn off.

She had some health problems (continual diarrhea for five months!) We had been told that Vietnamese babies couldn't tolerate milk, and we tried everything else, but she couldn't take any of it. Finally, Ray suggested in desperation that we try a little milk, and that worked! (The agency in Colorado had actually warned us that this condition often persisted in Vietnamese babies.)

Very soon, she became much stronger, babbling, eventually laughing. She loved being carried by our older daughter, who was age seven, or by any of the neighborhood kids, who doted on her. (We lived in a Black neighborhood.)

We moved to Athens when she was two years old. She did have to stay back a grade in 3rd grade. Her development probably suffered from the time in the orphanage. She was a favorite at the Green Acres community swimming pool, here in Athens. She refused to take swimming lessons at age five, but just taught herself, by imitating the older kids and their strokes. She was very strong and talented, and became a state-level swimming competitor.

In middle school and high school, she had problems with other Black girls, who were jealous of her long black hair, and because she was pretty. They sometimes threatened her, and she would pretend illness to stay home from school.

At age 14, she began trying to be "Black," by hanging out around the Nellie B area at night and dressing in sleazy clothes. Ray would drive around and find her, and bring her home. She also had serious problems with older boys who thought she was older, too.

We took her to a psychologist, who suggested modeling lessons in Atlanta to help her with self esteem, poise, clothing, etc. My caring husband drove her there for each lesson, and it was a great success. The psychologist also suggested letting her get a horse. (He loved to spend other people's money!) The horse worked miracles for her. She spent time taking riding lessons and caring for the horse, and spent that time with an older girl who was an excellent role model. That person happened to be Laura Carter, now a member of the band "Elf Power." Kathleen also excelled at riding competitions and winning ribbons. Again, my husband drove her to all of those activities. Unfortunately, my job as an HIV/AIDS educator and activist was just beginning to take all my time. And, I was _really_ scared of horses!

In high school, her gymnastics skills led her to be a varsity cheerleader, for football and basketball games.

Later, after high school, Kathleen tried several job-training programs, but nothing worked out. She found work as a receptionist for UGA Disability Services, and coincidentally, was diagnosed with ADD (Attention Deficit Disorder) herself. Later, she waitressed at Sonny's BBQ and told uproarious stories of fat families coming in after church with large numbers of misbehaving children, ordering "all you can eat," and then leaving ten-cent tips.

She eventually moved to South Beach, Miami, Florida, which she loved, and found a job as hostess at an upscale restaurant. She still loves the restaurant business (with all its problems and poor pay!)

As an adult, Kathleen was able to join a group of former orphans, sponsored by the agency that had helped in her adoption, for a trip back to Viet Nam, traveling from South to North, seeing both the beauty and the problems of the country, visiting the orphanages where she had been, and even meeting the ancient Vietnamese nun who had signed her birth certificate.

Finally, eight years ago, when my husband was dying of ALS (Lou Gehrig's Disease), Kathleen moved back home temporarily to help care for him. She said she wanted to give back, after all the care he had given to her.

Nancy MacNair

Destination Vacation
by Jim Marshall

When you travel to another country, you are generally expected to prepare a narrative about your journey for family and friends. Like every other genre, there are conventions governing these narratives; rules to be followed. For instance, it can't be too long—10 or 15 minutes at the outside. Photos can be included, but not too many. Slide shows tend to go long. You are required to dilate on the three most interesting things you saw (museums, castles, and Eiffel Tower-ish landmarks are always a good choice here). And best meal. You only get one so it's smart to choose lavishly expensive or charming and cheap. Most colorful character you met (lots of people default to a waiter), and most embarrassing moment. (The usual favorite is getting lost on the subway. It's always a knee slapper.)

The trouble with these narratives, no matter how well they are crafted, is that they tend to leave out the most important part of travel. And that is what happens between the notable moments that scaffold our stories. The journeys between destinations often provide lessons that the destinations themselves can't deliver. Let me explain with an example.

Peg and I spent the month of September travelling through the Northwestern coast of France. We visited four small towns—a week in each—in Normandy, Brittany, and the Loire Valley, travelling by train from one to the next. It was a glorious trip, the best travel we've ever had, and we fell in love with the country. But I want to talk about just one day.

It was a Saturday and we were moving from La Baule in southern Brittany to Amboise in the Loire Valley. It was a three-train trip with two short layovers to change trains. During the first leg, when we stopped at a small station, there was a booming announcement over the PA system. Of course, since we didn't speak French, we didn't know what was being said. But we did see that everyone around us was looking angry or at least annoyed and that they were gathering their luggage and moving toward the doors. We sat still in our ignorance until we decided to follow the others. We stopped on the platform and tried to figure out what to do. When a gentleman who was near us heard our English he realized why we were confused. "Ah," he said. "These things are always so irritating, so disruptive. The train has called a strike." Our confusion turned rapidly into dismay. We imagined that a strike meant a countrywide strike, and that our travel plans were doomed for the rest of our stay. But the gentleman saw our worry, and quickly calmed us by saying, "Don't worry. There is another train going to your destination. It's leaving in 15 minutes at another gate. I'm going there myself. I'll take you." And so he did, delivering us to the right gate and the right car, and then disappearing into the crowd without waiting for our thanks.

It was, in fact, a train going to our next layover, but it was not an express; it was a local, stopping at every village along the way. So we were late for the train we were to take next. The tickets we had for the third leg of the trip were useless, and the station where we landed had no counters where we could explain our situation and make alternative arrangements. We were quite completely stumped about what to do next. But my intrepid wife knew she could find an answer. She told me to stay in the station lobby with the luggage and then marched back into the terminal. After asking several train agents if they spoke English, she finally found one who did and explained where she could take the useless tickets to exchange them for another train. He could tell that she was already feeling lost and didn't want to have to ask for directions. So like the gentleman who earlier led us to a new train, this gentlemen led Peg to the well-hidden office where she exchanged our old tickets for new ones that would take us to our final destination. We were deeply relieved, and I was rightly proud of my wife's grit and persistence.

So we arrived in Amboise, a little late, but safely there. All we had to do was catch a taxi to our hotel. The train dropped us off at a gate that was on the opposite side of the tracks from the main entrance to the station, and to get there you had to go down a long cement staircase, through a tunnel, and then up another staircase. These staircases were not made for quasi-septuagenarian travellers, especially those carrying rolling suitcases and two heavy carry-ons, each containing digital devices, guidebooks, power cords, and dirty underwear. There were no handrails on the stairs, so we had to make two trips down and two up. But we got to the other side and looked around for a taxi stand. There didn't seem to be one. We went inside and asked about taxis and were handed a list of five phone numbers. Most did not answer and the others said they couldn't possibly come. Taxis in the small town had to be booked at least 24 hours in advance. We didn't have a clue as to where our hotel was, so Peg started approaching cars that were picking up people from arriving trains to show them the hotel's address and ask if they could provide directions. But no one spoke enough English to understand the question and our French was nonexistent. Finally, Peg approached a woman who did speak English. When Peg asked her about the hotel, the woman said, "I know exactly where it is. Let me pick up my daughter and I will take you there." At which point, she got out of the car, put our suitcases in the trunk and moved her 20-year-old dog into the front seat with her. Her daughter got in the car, looked warily back at us, and said something to her mother that we were sure would translate as, "Are you crazy?" But she was not; she was simply kind. She dropped us off at the front door of our hotel. We lamely tried to give her some money, but she refused, of course. "Do it for someone else sometime. Someone you don't know." And then she was off.

This could have turned out as the worst day of our time in France. But that night at dinner we toasted it as the best day. Three panicky, uncertain moments, each resolved by the undeserved, unlooked-for kindness of strangers. The gentleman who explained the strike to us and led us to our train, the train official who walked Peg to the office where she exchanged our tickets, and the lovely woman who drove us generously to our hotel. We didn't know when we left that morning that we were to arrive at three oases of grace, but we did. And that was the best destination of all.

Jim Marshall

On Her Own
By Janet Martin

My mother was 84 when her third husband, Herm, died. She had changed a lot from the woman who married my father at age 24. At that age she lacked confidence in herself and believed that men were superior beings to women. She deferred to my father's judgment on most things. When my father died it didn't take long for her to remarry. She married Don, a cocky man who enjoyed impressing others with his knowledge of wine, food and literature. I was not impressed, and it didn't take long for the shine to wear off the relationship. After about six months the marriage was annulled. In her late fifties she married for the third and last time. Herm was a gregarious man who had a great sense of humor. From my vantage point they had lots of good times together. However, he was often controlling and difficult. He developed Parkinson's in his early 70s. He did quite well for about ten years, but life became increasingly difficult for him and my mother as the disease rapidly progressed in his 80s. I saw a change in my mother. Herm became dependent on her and with that her confidence increased and she became more powerful. This also created problems in their relationship because Herm resented not being the person in charge as he once was. As he lost control over his body and his wife he became bitter and angry. He took these feelings out on my mother. After Herm died at age 84, my mother was not in the least bit interested in pursuing a relationship with another man. She rejected overtures from men, even when it was a friendly conversation, if she thought they might have other ideas. She told me, "Men are only interested in one thing!" This made me smile; we were talking about 80- and 90-year-olds, not 22-year-olds! She had had enough of men! Toward the end of her life she told me, "I didn't do a good job in choosing husbands."

Mom thrived living by herself. She stayed in her condominium in Sarasota. For the first time, her life revolved around her, not around parents, a husband or children. She did what she wanted to do. Despite minor health problems, she had no difficulty living independently. She enjoyed cooking for herself. She drove a car until she was 88. Bridge was the focal point of her life. She played duplicate bridge four times a week. She took bridge very seriously. She was quite competitive. At her memorial service, a number of her bridge cronies told me she was a very good bridge player. I was pleased to hear that. She and a friend had season tickets to a local theater company. She prided herself on her independence and was proud that she was able to live on her own. She had a minimal amount of help in the house. There was someone who cleaned her condo, and someone else who came in a few hours a week to do some of the chores she couldn't do.

Approximately once a month one of her three daughters would come and visit. She looked forward to these visits and planned activities in advance. We would go out to eat, see a play or concert and go shopping. It was so much fun to spend time with her. I looked forward to these visits as much as she did. She often said her daughters were the most important thing in her life. While we were growing up Mom was often stressed and during these times she could be difficult. In her later years she calmed down a good deal and it was enjoyable to spend time with her. Sometimes the old Mom behaviors came out when she was stressed, but not very often.

Her girls also made frequent phone calls to her. I called her about three or four times a week. She looked forward to our "after dinner" calls. I enjoyed settling in a comfortable chair and having us each share the events of our day.

Giving up her car was an adjustment for her. She had loved the independence the car gave her. She always said she would give up the car when she felt she was no longer a good driver. She actually thought she was a better driver than we daughters did, but we bided our time in telling her this. An unfortunate incident at the gas station led to her decision to give up driving. She had filled her car with gas and began to drive away from the pump. She somehow lost control of the car and drove into the gas pump, which proceeded to topple over. She was humiliated. She called each of her daughters to tell the tale and announce that she was giving up driving. The incident cost her insurance company $50,000. I know they were glad to get her off their rolls!

Mom wasted no time in finding a driver. One of her bridge buddies was willing to drive her where she needed to go. They worked out a financial arrangement. I was a bit apprehensive when Mom told me that 86-year-old Barbara would be her driver. She assured me that Barbara was a wonderful driver. This change in lifestyle turned out to be a blessing in disguise. Mom and Barbara became best friends. Barbara was a widow also. She lived with her older sister. She was full of energy and she and Mom had fun doing activities together.

To me Mom was a wonderful model of aging. She enjoyed life, even the mundane activities like grocery shopping and maintaining her home. She said she felt at peace and did not fear death. She died at age 90. I wish we could have kept her with us longer. Her death was an unfortunate accident. She got off the treadmill to answer the phone. She was waiting on a call from a prospective bridge partner. This was a high-priority call! When she got back on the treadmill she accidentally turned it to a high speed. She fell off onto the floor. She called 911 and the paramedics arrived. They took her to the hospital where she was examined and released. The paramedics had told her not to take her morning medicine before she went. They gave her medicine at the hospital and gave her a blood pressure pill that lowered her blood pressure too much. When she arrived at her front door, she fainted and hit her head on the concrete walk. Barbara was standing right next to her but was not able to stop her fall. Barbara called the daughters to report what had happened. I told Mom she should go to the hospital. She insisted she was fine. After two hours it became clear she was not fine, and she did go to the hospital. She was diagnosed with a subdural hematoma. She never left the hospital. She died about three weeks later on November 29, 2014. Her death has left a hole in my heart. I miss her every day. I constantly think about things I want to ask her or tell her about. I feel lucky to have had her for my mom.

Janet Martin
1-6-2020

Ours Is a Literate Family
by JES Mason

Ours is a literate family. When young Joseph Groff negotiated to buy the farm near Perrysville, Ohio, in 1821, he and his wife, Elizabeth, asked in every letter about the presence of a school and Mr. Darling assured them his wife was a capable teacher. She must have been. Joseph's oldest son, Elias, served as Township Supervisor for many years when that was an important position.

Their daughter Elizabeth married J.C. Sample, a largely self-educated man. He went to Nebraska to help found a college that was later made part of the University of Nebraska. He returned to a teaching position near Zelienople, PA. A group of businessmen hired J.C. to come to Perrysville to start a boys' prep school, the Greentown Academy, located on the Green Line dividing Indians and Whites. There he made quick work of meeting and marrying Elizabeth, a land-rich woman who soon inherited the Groff farm, henceforth known as the Sample Farm.

Their youngest among four daughters, my grandmother, Naomi Sample Jewett, studied at home as did all four sisters. J.C. couldn't let them attend the Greentown Academy. They studied the classics – Greek, Latin, and English languages and literature. She went from home schooling to Ohio State. That's not unusual now but at the time, the first decade of the 20th century, it was uncommon.

(Her transcript shows her college grades were not all that good.)

Naomi married Edwin Jewett, a veterinary student at OSU, and they had two daughters, both of whom went to Oberlin College for their degrees. My Aunt Elizabeth was brilliant. She graduated at 16 – from college – and was teaching high school Latin and English to students sometimes older than she was. My English major mother, Margaret, considered herself an OK student but did quite well in math and economics.

There was no question that my brother, my sister, and I would all go to college. You can see it was a family requirement.

A literate family requires desks – lots of desks. Our oldest is the Farm Desk. An itinerant carpenter built it on the farm about 1830 using walnut, cherry, poplar, and oak from trees felled on the Groff/Sample farm. One year the carpenter helped fell the trees and sawed them into boards stacked for a year to dry straight. The next year the boards had cured enough to use and the furniture was built. The Farm Desk is a massive secretary with a walnut case and a cherry lid that swings down to become a writing surface. It has a high stool so when I used it I always felt as though I had fallen into *David Copperfield, A Christmas Carol,* or some other story that included clerks in green eye shades perched at high desks.

Originally, the Farm Desk resided in the attic of the farm's kitchen. It would be a warm place to work in the winter but beastly hot in the summer.

There was only a ladder on the wall to get to the tiny room. I suppose a farmer does not much use his desk on hot summer days when he needs to be outdoors working the farm. Elias Groff used it when he was Township Supervisor, stuffing its many cubbyholes with letters and bills and its drawers with ledgers and records. Then my Great Uncle Joe ran the farm accounts from it and slept in the kitchen attic as well.

The Farm Desk became my Great Aunt Rua's desk after building the Pleasant Hill Dam drowned the farm. She used it to run her business, a school and dressmaking shop, training young women to become dressmakers and seamstresses. When Rua died, my mother inherited it and it was in the master bedroom in our small house in Toledo.

When we moved to Samaria, Michigan, I had a large room of my own and the Farm Desk came to me. I was in high school so I needed a larger desk. Now, the Farm Desk is with my daughter Lenea and she will, in time, pass it on to my grandson, Sam. How many generations is that? Elias to Joe, to Rua, to Mother, to me, to Lenea, to Sam makes seven.

Another old family desk is the Breakfront, a small walnut secretary with a tall glass-door bookcase built onto it (the 'breakfront'). Its age – late 19th century – as well as its compact size and tall bookcase tells me J.C. Sample bought it for his Headmaster's office at the Greentown Academy. When J.C. retired, the Breakfront came to the farm and then became Naomi's desk, then my mother's, then my brother's. His daughter Maureen now has it in her home. Five generations.

The mahogany Spinet Desk is newer. Built about 1925, it seems a likely gift for my brilliant Aunt Elizabeth as her college desk. I used it from the time I was in grade school. It was the envy of both my brother and sister for its cubbyholes, 'secret' compartments, and drawers. When I got the Farm Desk, Lance got the Spinet Desk and was overjoyed to get it.

It returned to me when he went to college. (He had a dorm room desk and I had a house.) By then, the Spinet Desk had been through two boys and had seen better days. The mahogany showed chips and scratches everywhere. I disassembled it and painted it very carefully, piece by piece – a really horrid antique blue on white. Still, it served us pretty well as a console table and returned to Lance when he finally had his own apartment with his second wife, Chris.

Disaster struck. A leg snapped off. Spinet desks were very common in the 1920s and into the 1930s. They are basically a big wooden box on long, spindly legs. Closed, they resemble a console table. The top folds back to reveal a writing surface, cubbyholes, and drawers. Figuring the long, spindly leg was beyond repair, Lance threw it out. I suspect it was the horrid blue antiquing that made the break convenient not to fix.

When eBay made it easy to locate relatively rare items, I started searching for a replacement. EBay listed a myriad of mahogany spinet desks priced from $200 to $5,000. None of them were 'my' Spinet Desk. I posted a 'wanted' ad with a description and I renewed it when it expired. We were spending summers at our home in Oregon, and winters in Georgia. I figured I would buy the 'right' desk no matter where we were when it showed up.

The exact replacement showed up after seven years and for a reasonable $400 price including the shipping. When it arrived at our Oregon house, it was perfect. Not a scratch – it looked brand new. The Spinet Desk went to my daughter Carrie in Oregon and she uses it as a console table. Presumably, it will go on to Victoria. Aunt Elizabeth, Mother, me, Lance, me again, Carrie, Victoria – six people across four generations.

The fourth family desk is the Butterfly Desk. Originally it belonged to the brilliant Elizabeth and came to my grandmother's apartment on Beth's sudden death. My mother inherited it. When Mother died, it was a desk so exquisite we had a family conference and gave it to my sister, Lynny. It is, after all, a very feminine desk. It is a classic maple writing desk from the 1930s with a felt insert on the slanted writing surface and a wooden breakfront hiding cubbyholes, drawers, and a small bookshelf. The breakfront doors each contain a large butterfly motif, hence its name. There are other decorative wood pieces that, taken together, make it way too decorative and feminine for a modern house. After Lynny died, Lance had it shipped to the Parish House, the B&B he and Chris ran. He replaced the felt with leather and the Butterfly Desk was given pride of place in their best room. Now, his daughter, Maureen, has it. Elizabeth to Margaret to Lynny to Lance to Maureen – five people across three generations.

Our own desks now are more modern and somewhat less convenient. We have five of them, none 'family' desks. What two people need with five desks is not easily explained. Their numbers grow, like Topsy. I wonder if any of these will enter the lists of family treasures. Maybe my glass and chrome one? Certainly not the inexpensive ones with sticking drawers and unattractive surfaces. The art of the desk has changed with computers and their requirements. But the old desks, the quality desks, will always be beautiful and functional and surprise youngsters with their secret drawers, mysterious cubbyholes, and wonderful possibilities.

© JES Mason

Comfort in the Time of the Pandemic
By JES Mason

There is comfort in the sound of an oscillating sprinkler.
Chure-r-r, Chure-r-r, Chure-r-r,
Whiker whack! Whicker whack! Whicker whack!
Chure-r-r, Chure-r-r, Chure-r-r,
Such a normal sound.
So common. So pedestrian,
Accompanied by bird-twitter, and,
In the far distance,
Traffic moving somewhere,
Going about its normal business.
Only birds visit my patio, birds and sun.
In the shade up the hill,
Lenten Roses droop under their load of man-made dew.
Farther down, Sun Drops glitter butter yellow,
The last of the Viola`stand up straight.
Iris fade, Coral Bells promise,
Lamb's Ear begins its spread.
Roses wait for their trim to put out new blooms.
A child's voice somewhere screeches delight.
An insect hums a quiet buzz.
Bluebird tends its brood.
Mocking Bird leaps high, singing all its music.
Mourning Dove cries for lost love.
All is normal.
All is a comfort.

s.s. devonshire 1851

by alice mohor

across the sea
cold deep and wide
our people came
to here abide

from british isles
and germany
the netherlands
and hungary

our storied lore
may well attest
but nothing like
the manifest

of the very
atlantic ship
with passengers
and date of trip

christmas stollen

by alice mohor

johannsmeier
her maiden name
from germany
her parents came

for holidays
grandmom would make
puddings and pies
cookies and cakes

christmas morning
we all would eat
german stollen
her special treat

a sugared bread
twice raised with yeast
spread with butter
our breakfast feast

sunday dinner
by alice mohor

roast leg of lamb
a special treat
pan potatoes
mint jelly sweet

cabbage salad
green english peas
brown gravy with
onion yes please

nana would serve
as plates would pass
candles burning
on mirrored glass

pop-pop would carve
to suit each guest
his knife and steel
the very best

OLLI@UGA

electric lawn mower

by alice mohor

always happy
to save some cash
dad brought it home
from curbside trash

broad sloping yard
with sprig size trees
whipping the cord
a jump rope breeze

easy enough
to cast the wire
till the saplings
grew much higher

more tedious
than had been known
when mowing where
the trees were grown

OLLI@UGA

35 mm slides

by alice mohor

thirty-six full
carousel trays
enough to view
for days and days

convention trips
vacation fun
playing outside
in summer sun

homecoming floats
circle line cruise
banquet dinners
picturesque views

holidays and
graduations
and birthdays all
celebrations

OLLI@UGA

old barney
by alice mohor

easter sunday
our first-time sight
of the famous
barnegat light

then in summer
a stair step feat
sometimes even
a race to beat

spiral climbers
pausing to stop
on their journey
to reach the top

where a lantern
once turned around
inside a prism
lens finely ground

Uncle Arthur Comes to Visit
by AC "Charles" Wilmoth

Arthur Balenger Young was my great-uncle. He was my maternal grandmother's brother and was known throughout the county as the shiftless, unemployed, bootlegging, backsliding, black sheep of our family. This was a mantle he wore easily and, to my thinking, with some pride. It is for these reasons, and a couple of others, that Arthur was, by far, my favorite uncle.

When I came into the family, he was in his late sixties. He had been married, then widowed, and had raised two boys. He had, for a short spell, held a steady job, but this was all before my time. Since then he had been unable to find work that inspired him and he had eked out a living by doing odd jobs, collecting scrap and making booze.

His work schedule allowed him time to come visit, something he did frequently. Our house was a convenient stop on his return home from one of his restocking runs. He lived across and just down the road from us; my dad said it was about a quarter of a mile. I enjoyed visiting with him and occasionally I would walk down to his house to see him. It was always an adventure as his house was very different from ours. It had four rooms built in a square and two big porches, one on the front and one on the back. It had a tin roof that roared when it rained and it had never been painted inside or out. The inside was piled high with fascinating collectibles my unappreciative mother referred to as "junk." There was a narrow walkway that wound through the house allowing access to necessities, such as appliances, a table and a bed, a bed whose sheets spoke to Arthur's lack of laundry skills.

The house sat in the middle of a large, fenced yard, which contained three other structures all in an advanced state of disrepair and also served as a pasture for two old horses. The yard behind the house was a tangle of briars, morning glories and honeysuckle. A well house butted right up against the back porch, providing access to a hand pump. There was an old, noxious outhouse nearly indistinguishable through the vines. Nearby was an old tool shed that doubled as a stable for the two horses. It was also host to a tangle of vines.

Within the confines of the fence, the horses were free to do as they pleased. One day when Arthur was gone, one of them climbed up on the front porch. As soon as the horse got all four feet up on the porch, the old boards under him collapsed. The animal fell through to the ground and was unable to extract himself until Arthur sawed out an escape path. Since the destruction did not hamper access to the front door, the porch was never repaired.

While I admired my uncle's relaxed attitude toward work, the thing I really liked about him was his yarn-spinning capability. It didn't take much prompting to get his creative juices flowing. Most folk questioned the veracity of his tales, but I didn't. I mostly believed his stories and I always tried to. One afternoon, we were standing in the yard when a small airplane flew overhead. Seeing my interest in it, he quickly conjured up a tale. In this story, he had been a pilot for the FBI and flew an aircraft just like the one that had just passed over us. His mission was to ferret out bootleggers operating in the area and to report their whereabouts to FBI headquarters. As I recall the narrative, he never mentioned whether or not he had surveilled his own house, which was the most obvious place in the county to find a bootlegger.

Arthur's most reliable source of income was his bootlegging enterprise. He was proud of his skill as a brewmaster. He made beer out of all sorts of fruits and vegetables, but he preferred sweet potatoes, which were plentiful and cheap. I don't remember much else about his beer-making process, but he used big crock containers and when he poured the brew from one container to another he would strain it through an old, soiled apron he wore. He would flip the apron up over the crock and pour the concoction through it. He never removed the apron while working and a strange-smelling liquid would drizzle all over the floor.

One day the local Baptist preacher stopped by our house to tell my mother he had just visited her uncle Arthur and he was very concerned about him. Arthur had told him he had been unable to attend services because he had been seriously ill. It was a lingering illness that kept him so weak he was often unable to leave the house. Even though he had not darkened the door of the church for several years, he insisted he still missed hearing a good sermon and assured the preacher he would be back as soon as he regained his strength. Arthur had not invited the preacher in, choosing instead to visit through the screen door. The preacher surmised it was to prevent him from being infected with the unknown illness. But perhaps it had more to do with the booze-soaked apron that was dripping on Arthur's shoes.

For transportation Arthur owned an old Chevrolet. It was a miracle of automotive engineering, having survived many years without service or shelter and had endured countless mishaps that had left it running but always with far less confidence. Once a dark blue, its paint now competed with rust to be the principal color of the car. The car only had one headlight and the taillights flickered to the rhythm of the bumps in the road. But its most remarkable characteristic was its interior. There were no seats, no upholstery, no gauges; there was only bare metal, a steering wheel and the three pedals required to operate the car. The gas gauge had been replaced by a long, limber stick that was used to fathom the depth of the gas in the tank. A speedometer was not required since Arthur always drove the car as fast as it would go, a speed that was unpredictable and alternated between sudden bursts of forward thrust and sputtering stalls.

Arthur had constructed a wooden box on which he sat when driving. It was a precarious perch, especially when the road was rough. He once crossed a railroad track, which was rougher than he figured and at a speed faster than he figured. The old car's suspension collapsed and rebounded, launching Arthur upward off the box, banging his head on the top of the car and sending him sprawling backward. The now driverless car bounced and careened down the road until it finally veered into the ditch, where a wrecker was required to extract it. Fortunately the only casualty of the accident was Arthur's hat.

It was the familiar sounds made by the old Chevrolet as it coughed and sputtered to life and started up the road that alerted us that Uncle Arthur was coming. We might not have heard it had we not had the windows open. It was a warm summer evening, just after dark. My dad had opened the windows hoping for a cooling breeze. We wondered if something was wrong because Arthur never ventured out at night. His night vision had been weakened by the passing years and by the homemade sleep aid he dosed himself with at night. So we knew he was coming to our house. My brother and I hurried outside to meet him.

The old car turned into our driveway and skidded to a grinding halt right beside us. Arthur opened the car door and fell as he got out. My brother and I helped him to his feet, and he held onto us briefly and then collapsed. Uncle Arthur had come to see us for the last time.

Arthur was true to his word; he returned to the little Baptist Church of his youth, just like he insisted he would. His service was conducted by the preacher who had expressed concern for Arthur's physical health. I figured he was now harboring concerns for the health of Arthur's eternal soul. But, I had no such thoughts about Arthur; he always seemed too busy enjoying the present to be creating problems in the hereafter. And I knew he could talk his way out of any difficulties he might encounter along the way. But I was still relieved when, during the benediction, I heard the familiar drone of a small airplane passing over the church and heading for the horizon. I closed my eyes and whispered, "God speed, Uncle Arthur."

AC "Charles" Wilmoth

OLLI@UGA

Under Thy Sheltering Arms
By DeAnne Wilmoth

This is a story about a tree, not just any tree, but a huge, flowering pear tree that stood in the front yard of my childhood home. This extraordinary tree became a symbol for all that was good about my childhood.

After a turbulent five years after the death of my Mother, my Father finally decided it was time to bring us to his childhood home in Arkansas. After three long days on the road from North Hollywood, California to Tull, Arkansas, my brother and I anxiously awaited our arrival. We chugged down a winding gravel road past farm after farm, cows grazing along the fences that dotted both sides of the road. We finally pulled up in front of a farmhouse I would learn to call home. I looked out the window to see a giant pear tree and under that tree sat my Grandma DuVall. After months of trauma and grief, we knew we were finally home. The scene is etched in my memory, the towering pear tree shading the face of my Grandmother as she waved to us from her chair.

The tree was swollen with new fruit, pears falling all over the ground. My Grandmother slowly rose from her chair and gathered me in her arms. My memory of that moment is imprinted in my heart and mind. The scent of overripe pears and Grandma's sweet scent remain with me these many years later.

The pear tree became the gathering place for my boisterous extended family. My Grandfather, E.H. DuVall, a staunch Yellow Dog Democrat, was a teacher and a state representative. Folks from our small community often stopped by to discuss the politics of the day. The tree heard many discussions from the many friends gathered there. Republicans and Democrats always "respectfully disagreed" on issues but would always leave with a handshake and a hearty goodbye. As a child I was fascinated by their heated discussions and boisterous laughter.

Many afternoons I napped on a quilt under that tree while my Grandma shelled peas or peeled pears. Spring and summer were filled with cousins visiting. The branches of that towering tree became horses we rode as we acted out cowboy movies we had seen. The limbs never broke under our weight but stood strong year after year and watched us grow into teenagers sneaking a kiss under those sheltering arms.

The end of summer brought the fruits of our tree: pear preserves, fat chunks of pears canned for a cold winter night, branches that fell to the ground that were gathered and used for the fireplace that warmed my bedroom. Many a night I went to sleep with the warmth of the fire to comfort me.

Sunday afternoons brought all the relatives to eat fried chicken, corn on the cob, purple hull peas and cornbread. An apple cobbler was a favorite made with apples from our own apple tree. I remember children running around our tree and listening to the family stories, stopping occasionally to sit on the lap of a favorite aunt.

The farm was sold when my Grandmother died and many families have come and gone since then, but now, 67 years later, the pear tree still stands with limbs that seem to reach the sky. Other children have played under her towering branches and I hope they too will remember the joy that the pear tree has brought to many generations. I pray that every child will learn to love a tree as I loved mine. The echo of all those voices under that beautiful tree will forever remind me of the overwhelming sense of love and belonging that has never left me, and today, all these many years later, I thank God for "those sheltering arms."

DeAnne Wilmoth

Made in the USA
Columbia, SC
03 July 2020